The Seven Key Aspects of SMSFs

View Legal

Matthew
Burgess

National Library of Australia Cataloguing-in-Publication entry

Author: Burgess, Matthew, author.
Title: The Seven Key Aspects of SMSFs / Matthew Burgess
ISBN: 9781925181494 (paperback)
Subjects: Pension trusts--Australia.
Pension trusts--Taxation--Australia.
Retirement income--Australia.
Estate planning--Australia.

Dewey Number: 331.2520994

Important disclaimer

This book covers legal and technical issues in a general way. It is not designed to express opinions on specific cases. This book is intended for information purposes only and should not be regarded as legal advice. Further advice should be obtained before taking action on any issue dealt with in this publication.

Table of Contents

Introduction ix
Acknowledgements x

Chapter 1
OVERVIEW OF THE FUNDAMENTAL ASPECTS OF SMSFS 1

Introduction 3
Glossary of abbreviations 4
Explanation of SMSFs 5
Structure overview 6
Trustee 7
Members 8
Trust deed 9
Investing via superannuation 10
SMSF PDS 12
Overview 13
SMSFs 14
Establishing an SMSF 16
Costs and cooling off period 19
Trustee and member eligibility 20
Investments 22
Restrictions on investments 24
Contributions 26
Payment of benefits 33
Preserved benefits 34
Death benefits 35
Taxation 37

Other information 42
Is the trust deed up to date? 46
Age of trust deed 47
Deeds of variation 48
SMSFs and separate bank accounts 50
Corporate trustees and SMSFs 52
Pensions and commutation 53
Reserves 54
Re-contribution strategy 55

Chapter Two
INVESTMENT BORROWING STRUCTURES 57

Overview 59
Relevant investment rules 61
Borrowings 65
Prohibition on charging assets 66
Prohibition on improving assets 67
IHA rule 68
SMSF borrowing arrangements and business succession 69
Geared Unit Trusts 74
What does 'sufficiently influenced' mean? 77
Section 71(4) - deemed IHA 79
Breach of IHA rules 80
Public Trading Trust rules 81

Chapter Three
ESTATE PLANNING AND ASSET PROTECTION 87

Overview 89
The role of the trustee 90
Trusteeship issues within an SMSF 91
Corporate trustees 94

Income stream overview 96
Estate Planning Costs Paid Through an SMSF 97
Refreshing of cost base 100
SMSFs and asset protection 102
Superannuation and bankruptcy 104
Notional estate provisions 106

Chapter Four
DEATH BENEFITS 109

Overview 111
Form of payment 114
Taxation of death benefits 115
Other considerations 118
Payments to the estate and testamentary trusts 122
CGT and death benefit in specie distributions 123
SPTs 125
SPTs established outside a will 127
Use of nominations 129
When should BDBN be used? 133
Superannuation wills 135
Reversionary pensions 137
Case law 139

Appendix One
MODEL SMSF TRUST DEED 147

Overview 149
Agreed terms 150
Schedule 1 - Powers of Trustee 197

Appendix Two

TEMPLATE INVESTMENT STRATEGY 209

Template Investment Strategy 211

1 Overview 211

2 Future Contributions 212

3 Past Investment Performance/Asset Mix 212

4 Investment Objectives 212

5 Investment Strategy 214

SIS Requirements 221

Prudential Requirements 223

Organisational Issues 224

Resources 225

Fees 226

Appendix Three

NON-BINDING DEATH BENEFIT NOMINATIONS 227

Nominated beneficiaries 229

Appendix Four

BINDING DEATH BENEFIT NOMINATIONS 231

Binding nomination 233

Appendix Five

INFORMATION SHEET - BDBN 237

Overview 239

About the Author 243

Introduction

Matthew Burgess, together with Patrick Ellwood, Naomi Arnold and Tara Lucke are co-founders, of View Legal.

Having previously founded Australia's first virtual law firm as a wholly owned subsidiary of one of the country's leading independent law firms, View Legal is result focused and passionate about delivering new solutions in a way that aligns with their 'SPS' – Service and Price Satisfaction – guarantee.

As an author, Matthew is a recognised expert, who constantly creates innovative strategies for the growth, management and protection of wealth.

He is published across a range of topics including:

1. The Nine Steps to a Complete Estate Plan;
2. The Seven Foundations of Business Succession;
3. The Seven Key Aspects of Testamentary Trusts;
4. The Nine Essential Blue Journal Articles;
5. Inside Stories – the complete collection of blog posts (2010-2014) and
6. The Six Foundations of the Taxation of Trusts.

Acknowledgements

Each member of the View Legal Team, in particular co-founders Naomi Arnold, Patrick Ellwood and Tara Lucke, have contributed to various aspects of this book. Thank you to each of them.

Chapter 1

OVERVIEW OF THE FUNDAMENTAL ASPECTS OF SMSFs

Introduction

IN RECENT YEARS, the need for effective structuring of retirement savings has been brought into sharp focus for private investors and business owners alike.

The combination of fundamental changes to the taxation regime, the vast amounts of wealth accumulated within superannuation funds, for many the perceived lack of value delivered by industry funds and the increasing tendency for both business and personal relationships to be relatively short term (as opposed to lifelong) have meant that traditional approaches to superannuation have been revolutionised.

In this context, the use of SMSFs has become ubiquitous.

The range of fundamental issues that need to be considered in relation to establishing and successfully maintaining an SMSF is vast.

This book analyses the key aspects of SMSFs, in the following order:

a glossary of abbreviations;
b explanation of the structure of trusts generally, with particular reference to SMSFs;
c overview of the fundamental aspects of SMSFs, using an example 'product disclosure statement' as the basis;
d analysis of the main SMSF investment structures, including use of borrowing;
e SMSFs, estate planning and asset protection;
f death benefit nominations;
g example SMSF trust deed, including comprehensive user notes;
h template SMSF investment strategy; and
i pro-forma SMSF nominations (both binding and non-binding).

Glossary of abbreviations

ABN–Australian Business Number
ASIC–Australian Securities and Investments Commission
ATO–Australian Taxation Office
ARP–auto reversionary pension
Bankruptcy Act–*Bankruptcy Act 1966* (Cth)
BDBN–binding death benefit nomination
CGT–capital gains tax
Corporations Act–The Corporations Act 2001 (Cth)
Disability Services Act–Disability Services Act 1986 (Cth)
GST–Goods and Services Tax
IHA–in-house asset
LPR–legal personal representative
PAYG–Pay As You Go
PDS–Product disclosure statement
SCT–Superannuation Complaints Tribunal
SG Act–*Superannuation Guarantee (Administration) Act 1992* (Cth)
SIS Act–*Superannuation Industry (Supervision) Act 1993* (Cth)
SIS Regulations–the regulations made under the SIS Act
SMSF–self managed superannuation fund
SPT–Superannuation Proceeds Trust
Tax Act–*Income Tax Assessment Act 1936* (Cth) and the *Income Tax Assessment Act 1997* (Cth) (together with regulations and public rulings issued under those Acts)
TFM–testator's family maintenance
TFN–Tax File Number
TRIS–Transition to Retirement Income Stream

Explanation of SMSFs

ARGUABLY THE BEST introduction to SMSFs is the PDS document that is required by legislation to be provided to any person considering the establishment, or becoming a member, of an SMSF.

Following the structure overview below, the balance of this chapter is largely based on a 'standard' PDS.

Many of the concepts mentioned in this chapter are explored in more detail elsewhere in the book, or the appendixes.

As with most areas of the law, superannuation rules, particularly for SMSFs, change regularly due to government and ATO driven legislation amendments and the impact of court decisions. Specialist and specific advice should always be obtained at the time of addressing any of the issues covered in this book.

Structure overview

A TRUST IS, IN effect, simply a legal relationship where there is:

a a legal owner of property (the 'trustee');
b who holds the property ('trust property');
c for the benefit of others (the 'beneficiaries'); and
d pursuant to certain terms or rules ('trust deed').

In the context of an SMSF, the key point of slight differentiation is that the 'beneficiaries' are referred to as 'members'.

Diagrammatically, the structure of an SMSF is represented below:

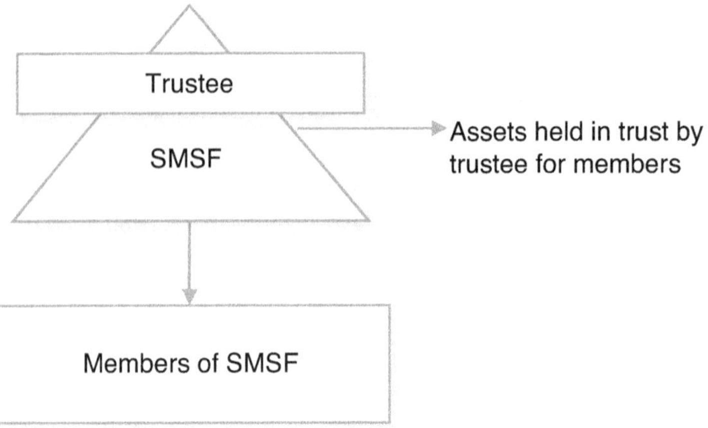

Trustee

The trustee is the legal owner of the property. The trustee will therefore have the ultimate control over the assets of the SMSF.

The trustee can be a company or one or more individuals, subject to rules set out under the SIS Act, as explained later in this book. Where the trustee is a company, the directors of the company will have the day-to-day control of the SMSF.

As the shareholders of the company appoint the directors, the shareholders will have the ultimate control over the SMSF, again however subject to the SIS Act rules.

Although the trustee is responsible for the day-to-day running of the SMSF, some deeds have a 'principal' (also commonly known as an appointor, guardian or nominator) who retains ultimate control over the SMSF. The principal has the ability to appoint and remove the trustee at any time, and its consent may be required to make any amendments to the trust deed.

If the trust deed does not name a principal, the existing trustee will usually have the power to appoint a new trustee.

Members

THE SMSF STRUCTURE enables income that is earned by the SMSF to be distributed to the members in accordance with their member balance, once a condition of release set out under the SIS Act is satisfied.

Trust deed

THE TRUST DEED of an SMSF sets out how the SMSF must be run, what the trustees can do in running the fund and who the members are.

The trust deed must comply with the provisions of the SIS Act.

It is necessary to review an SMSF trust deed periodically to ensure that it allows the trustees to operate the fund in effective way and in accordance with the current legislation.

Unlike most other forms of trusts, SMSFs do not have a 'vesting day' (or ending day). Generally non SMSF trusts can last for a maximum period of 80 years.

Investing via superannuation

A THRESHOLD ISSUE IN relation to SMSFs is whether wealth should be invested outside of the superannuation environment, for example, by reducing personal debt as opposed to making contributions to superannuation.

This decision will be affected by any array of variables, including:

a the member's current income and marginal tax rate;
b the member's existing assets and liabilities and the interest rates on borrowings;
c the risk profile of the member and what the intended investments inside and outside superannuation are likely to be (and therefore the potential investment returns of each investment);
d the age of the member, the time frame until they are able to access their superannuation (i.e. their preservation age) and whether they would be looking to retire earlier than their preservation age;
e whether the member has any dependants; and
f the security of the member's employment.

Factors in favour of superannuation investments

A summary of the factors that would support investment via superannuation include where the member:

a is nearing preservation age and intends to retire meaning that there is only a short period of time between when they make the contributions and when they are able to access their entitlements;
b has a high personal tax rate and is eligible to make salary sacrifice or personal contributions to reduce the tax payable;

c. believes the investment earnings are likely to outperform, for example, interest rates on any borrowings loans; and
d. is able to service debt.

Factors in favour of non-superannuation investments

A summary of the factors that would support investment outside the superannuation regime include where the member:

a. is close to exceeding the limits imposed on contributions;
b. wants to acquire investments which are of a value that the contributions caps would prevent the purchase;
c. does not have any tax dependants – investing outside superannuation would allow those assets to pass tax free to non-dependants on the member's death;
d. is looking to retire or otherwise have access savings prior to preservation age and therefore have access to investments earlier than permitted via superannuation;
e. finds the superannuation laws, particularly in relation to SMSFs, unduly complex and subject to change too frequently;
f. wants to invest with related parties without any restriction.

SMSF PDS

Summary

Purpose of PDS

This summary is designed to help you make a decision about whether to acquire an interest in an SMSF (**fund**).

The Law allows you 14 days from the date of issue of the PDS to decide if you wish to acquire an interest in the fund.

Information in a PDS

The PDS generally sets out:

a the nature of SMSF;
b the main advantages and disadvantages of acquiring an interest in the fund; and
c information about contributions, payment of benefits and related tax issues.

What you should do

If you decide to acquire an interest in the fund please sign and date the PDS.

Overview

THIS PDS IS intended to be a general guide in relation to establishing and maintaining an SMSF. It is not intended to be legal or financial advice.

If you intend to take action (or not act) based on something dealt with in this PDS, you should firstly obtain specialist advice. Advice can generally be provided by any specialist financial adviser, accountant, or lawyer.

The PDS provides general commentary about SMSFs, including:

a their advantages and disadvantages;
b contributions;
c payment of benefits; and
d taxation issues.

SMSFs

An SMSF is a superannuation fund with four or less members established by a trust deed. The members of an SMSF have sole responsibility to manage the fund. In contrast, larger funds have an independent trustee who is responsible for all aspects of managing the fund.

Advantages and disadvantages

The main advantages and disadvantages of an SMSF, are outlined below.

The advantages of an SMSF can include:

a trustees have the discretion to choose the investments of the fund, within its investment;
b ability to borrow to buy assets;
c generally a maximum 15% tax rate on income and a 10% tax rate on capital gains;
d generally a 0% tax rate for members aged at least 60 receiving on income stream;
e flexibility on tailoring how members receive benefits, including using TRIS;
f complementary estate planning arrangements using benefit nominations;
g flexibility in relation to insurance arrangements;
h intergenerational wealth management (subject to the maximum member limit of 4 members);
i tax-free payments when the member dies to their 'tax dependants' (explained below);
j ability to transfer assets to members 'as is' (or 'in specie'), instead of being sold and the cash distributed;

k asset protection on a member's bankruptcy;
l reduced reporting requirements when compared with larger funds; and
m ability to potentially access a lower fee structure than that for larger funds.

Depending on your circumstances, many of the advantages outlined above may in fact be disadvantages.

Some other specific disadvantages of an SMSF can include:

a the amount of personal involvement, responsibility and specialised knowledge required to manage the fund;
b fees can be greater than those for larger funds, particularly if the SMSF has a small asset base;
c once established, it can be difficult to unwind an SMSF, particularly if its assets are illiquid; and
d there are strict Australian residency rules for members.

Establishing an SMSF

THE MAIN STEPS to establish an SMSF are summarised below.

Trust deed

A document confirming the rules by which the trustee administers the SMSF must be prepared (trust deed). All trustees are bound by the trust deed and are jointly responsible for any breach of it.

The deed must be dated, signed by each trustee and updated regularly for changes in the law.

Trustee eligibility

An individual trustee, or a director of a corporate trustee must be:

a at least 18 years of age; and
b not an undischarged bankrupt, insane or a 'disqualified person'.

A person will be a 'disqualified person' if they are:

a insolvent;
b convicted of an offence relating to dishonest conduct at any time; or
c subject to a civil penalty order for breaches of the superannuation laws.

Trustees

The trustees manage the SMSF and must be either a company or individuals. For constitutional reasons where there are individual trustees, the purpose of the SMSF must be the provision of old age pensions.

A sole purpose company acting as trustee is generally seen as best practice as it:

a allows greater certainty and control because companies can exist indefinitely;
b gives access to lower annual ASIC lodgement fees as compared to other companies; and
c ensures fewer administrative costs when control of the SMSF changes. For example, the removal or admission of an individual trustee means title to each asset of the fund must be changed. For a corporate trustee, all that is required when changing a director is a notice to ASIC. Title in the assets of the fund remains in the name of the corporate trustee.

Election

To access the concessional taxation regime, the trustee of an SMSF must lodge an election with the ATO within 60 days of establishing the fund.

Applications for TFN, ABN and GST

Trustees must lodge an 'Application to Register for the New Tax System Superannuation Entity' form to obtain a TFN, ABN and, if necessary, to register for the GST.

Specific steps may also be required to ensure compliance with:

a PAYG obligations;
b withholding tax; and
c various state taxes.

Standards of care

There are a number of minimum standards of care imposed on every trustee of an SMSF, including acting:

a honestly;
b prudently;

c. in the best interests of members; and
d. in accordance with the standards of care prescribed under the superannuation laws.

Any breach of these standards of care can trigger civil and criminal penalties.

Bank account

A trustee must establish a bank account to hold all money belonging to an SMSF separate from other accounts (for example from members, the trustee personally and from contributing employers).

Any cheques paid to an SMSF should be clearly marked, for example, 'XYZ Pty Ltd as trustee for the SMSF Fund'.

Any investments by an SMSF should be similarly recorded.

Remuneration

Trustees cannot be paid for performing their trustee duties in managing an SMSF.

Costs and cooling off period

Costs

There are numerous costs associated with operating an SMSF, including:

a legal fees establishing the fund;
b accounting fees in preparing regulatory returns and administering the fund;
c transaction costs in relation to acquiring and maintaining assets; and
d ongoing management costs (including audit fees on an annual basis).

The quantum of fees can vary between firms and best practice involves considering the likely costs prior to deciding to establish an SMSF.

Cooling off period

This PDS is designed to help you decide whether to acquire an interest in an SMSF.

The Law allows you 14 days from the date of issue of this PDS to decide if you want to proceed.

It is important to note that during this cooling off period you have the right to decide not to acquire an interest in an SMSF.

Trustee and member eligibility

SPECIFIC RULES APPLY to admission as a trustee or member of an SMSF depending on issues such as whether the SMSF has:

a individual trustees;
b a corporate trustee; or
c is a single member fund.

Individual trustees

Where an SMSF has individual trustees:

a the fund can only have a maximum of four members;
b each individual trustee must be a member of the fund and vice versa; and
c no member can be an employee of another member of the fund, unless they are related.

Corporate trustee

Where an SMSF has a corporate trustee, essentially the same rules as those for an SMSF controlled by individual trustees apply, however each director of the trustee company must be a fund member and vice versa.

Single member

Where an SMSF has a single member, the SMSF must satisfy one of the following rules:

a it must have a corporate trustee of which the member is the sole director;
b it must have a corporate trustee of which the member is one of only two directors and the other director is either a relative, or

a person who is not a relative and also not an employer, of the member; or

c two individual trustees, one of whom is the member and the other is either a relative, or a person who is not a relative and also not an employer, of the member.

Exceptions

The trustee and member rules are subject to the following main exceptions:

a a parent or guardian can act as trustee or director for a member under 18;

b where a member is deceased or incapacitated, a LPR can act as trustee for that member;

c a beneficiary of a pension paid following a member's death is considered a member of the fund if that beneficiary is not already a member (and therefore must become a trustee or if the trustee is a company, a director of the trustee); and

d a person holding an enduring power of attorney for an incapacitated member can act as a trustee or director for a member without formally being a member.

Investments

Sole purpose test

SMSFs must comply with the 'sole purpose test' in the SIS Act to avoid significant penalties.

This means all investment of the fund must be acquired for the sole purpose of providing retirement benefits for members and also comply with various investment rules.

Written investment strategy

Before acquiring any investment, an SMSF must have a written investment strategy taking into account issues such as cash flow, risk, return, diversification, liquidity and ability of the fund to meet liabilities when they arise.

The investment risk profiles of each individual member of the SMSF must also be considered. For example, it might be appropriate that members nearing retirement have a higher proportion of their funds invested in low risk, capital preserving investments.

A financial adviser or investment manager holding an Australian Financial Services Licence should be engaged if the trustee requires any guidance about an SMSF's investment strategy.

An SMSF investment strategy must be reviewed and updated regularly.

A template example investment strategy is set out in the appendix to this book.

Types of investments

An SMSF can generally invest in any form of assets including shares, bonds, property, and cash. However speculative investments, even in traditional asset classes (for example share futures trading) may not be considered a prudent investment in the context of the 'sole purpose test' outlined above.

The ATO also generally considers certain 'lifestyle' related investments (for example, cars, boats, beach houses and artwork) that can be enjoyed, leased or used personally by fund members or their related parties as inappropriate investments.

Specialist advice should be obtained before investing in a manner that does not clearly align with the sole purpose test and an agreed investment strategy.

Restrictions on investments

THERE ARE A number of restrictions on the types of investments an SMSF may make. The main rules are set out below.

OVERVIEW

An SMSF cannot lend money or otherwise provide financial assistance to members or related parties.

An SMSF can only borrow money if:

a the lender complies with the limited recourse loan provisions;
b it relates to the settlement of share transactions within 7 days and the value of the transaction is less than 10% of the value of the fund;
c the borrowing helps fund benefit payments and the amount borrowed is less than 10% of the value of the fund and is for less than 90 days.

An SMSF should ensure all transactions are on arm's length terms.

SPECIFIC CONSTRAINTS

An SMSF must ensure less than 5% of the market value of its assets are invested in IHAs. IHAs include investments in, loans to or a lease arrangement with a related party.

Related parties include fund members and their associates (such as relatives, business partners and entities controlled by a member or their associates).

Importantly, the prohibition on an SMSF acquiring assets from a member or a related party does not apply to:

a listed shares;
b business real property (as defined in the SIS Act);
c interests in a widely held unit trust; or

d. interests in a closely held unit trust where there are no borrowings.

Specialist advice should be obtained before seeking access to any of the above exceptions.

Contributions

CONTRIBUTIONS TO AN SMSF can generally be made by:

a an employer of a member;
b a member; and
c the spouse of the member.

The quantum of concessional contributions permitted in a financial year is subject to a limit for each employee that contributions are made for.

Concessional contributions which count towards the concessional limit include all employer contributions (e.g. super guarantee and salary sacrifice), member contributions which are claimed as a tax deduction and certain allocations from fund reserves.

The amount of non-concessional member contributions is also subject to annual limits.

Self employed

Self-employed people are ineligible for tax deductions for superannuation contributions if more than 10% of their income is earned as an employee.

A self-employed person wishing to claim a tax deduction for concessional contributions must notify the trustee in writing and receive an acknowledgement.

Under 65

Anyone under the age of 65 can make contributions without restrictions.

Between the ages of 65 and 74

Contributions from a person aged 65 to 74 can be made if the person has been gainfully employed on at least a part time basis during the financial year.

The specific definition in this regard is that the person worked at least 40 hours over a period of not more than 30 consecutive days in the financial year.

Over 75

A person cannot make personal superannuation contributions from 28 days after the end of the month in which they turn 75.

Under 18

Persons under the age of 18 are entitled to a deduction for contributions if they have derived income from the carrying on a business or from eligible employment.

Contribution limits

The maximum amount of concessional and non-concessional contributions that may be paid by an employer, a self-employed person or a member for the 2015/2016 year of income without potentially being subject to excess contributions tax, is set out below:

Contribution type	Contribution limit
Concessional contributions	$30,000 per annum per person under 49 years on 30 June 2015 $35,000 per annum per person aged 49 years and over on 30 June 2015
Non-concessional contributions	$180,000 per annum per person (for contributions on or after 1 July 2014) $540,000 per person under 65 averaged over three years (if a 3 year contribution was started before 1 July 2014 then the limit is $450,000)

For any excess superannuation contributions made after 1 July 2013 breaching the non-concessional cap, the government will allow individuals to withdraw those excess contributions and associated earnings.

If a member chooses this option, no excess contributions tax will be payable and any related earnings will be taxed at their marginal tax rate.

As is well understood, concessional contributions to superannuation can generally be made by:

a an employer of a member;
b a member; and
c the spouse of the member.

The rules in relation to the quantum of permissible concessional contributions (historically referred to as deductible contributions) have been subject to regular change. The changes have primarily focused on the dollar limit for contributions made in each financial year.

Concessional contributions which currently count towards the annual concessional limit include:

a all employer contributions (e.g. super guarantee, salary sacrifice);
b member contributions which are claimed as a tax deduction; and
c in some situations, allocations from any fund reserves.

A table summarising how non-concessional contributions can potentially be 'accelerated' is set out below. The table assumes that the first contribution is made after 1 July 2014.

If a combined contribution is commenced before this date the references to $180,000 should be replaced with $150,000 and the references to $540,000 should be replaced with $450,000.

Contributions can be less than the maximum deductible contribu-

Member age	61	62	63	64	65	
Financial year	2014/15	2015/16	2016/17	2017/18	2018/19	Total Contributions
Scenario 1	$180,000	$180,000	$180,000	$180,000	$180,000[1]	$900,000
Scenario 2	$180,000	$180,000	$540,000	nil	nil	$900,000
Scenario 3	$180,000	$180,000	$180,000	$540,000	nil	$1,080,000
Scenario 4	$540,000	nil	nil	$540,000	nil	$1,080,000
Scenario 5	$180,000	$540,000	nil	nil	$540,000[2]	$1,260,000
Scenario 6	$180,000	$180,000	$180,000	$180,000	$540,000[1]	$1,260,000

[1]Assuming contributions are made prior to member's 65th birthday or made after reaching age 65 and the member continues to satisfy the required gainful employment test.
[2]Assuming contributions are made prior to member's 65th birthday or the member was aged 65 at any time in the year and continues to satisfy the required gainful employment test or the contributions were made after the member's 65th birthday.

tions and any contributions made should be credited to a member's accumulation account within 28 days of the end of the month they are received.

Spouse contributions

Where a spouse is a member of the fund, eligible spouse contributions may be accepted by an SMSF at any time if the spouse is under the age of 65.

If the spouse is aged 65 to 74, eligible spouse contributions may only be accepted if the spouse is gainfully employed on at least a part time basis. If the spouse is 75 or over, no spouse contributions can be made.

Contributions for children under 18

Parents, grandparents, friends and employers can contribute on behalf of children.

Co-contribution for low income earners

Subject to a Government proposal to repeal the co-contribution scheme, if a person makes a personal super contribution, the Government will make a co-contribution up to certain limits on the following basis (current to 30 June 2016):

Lower income threshold	Higher income threshold	Co-contribution	Maximum entitlement
$35,454	$50,454	$0.50 for every $1, up to a maximum super co- contribution limit of $500 a year	The maximum entitlement is $500. However, this is reduced by 3.333 cent for every dollar of total income, less business deductions over $35,454, up to $50,454.

Minimum employer contributions

Employers must contribute a minimum amount of superannuation support for each employee as set out in the SG Act.

The minimum amount progressively contributed by an employer is 9% to 12% between 1 July 2012 and 1 July 2019. The rate is 9.5% from 1 July 2014 and will remain at this level until 30 June 2018. The rate will then increase by 0.5 percentage points each year until it reaches 12% in 2022/23.

Contributions on behalf of directors of corporate trustees

One further issue that often arises is whether the corporate trustee of a family trust can claim a tax deduction for the super contributions paid on behalf of a director to a complying superannuation fund?

A taxpayer is entitled to a deduction for a contribution it makes to a superannuation fund for the purpose of providing superannuation benefits for another person who is the taxpayer's employee when the contribution is made.

For this purpose, an employee includes both an individual who is either an employee under common law or an employee within the expanded meaning under the SG Act.

The expanded definition of 'employee' treats a person who is entitled to payment for the performance of duties as a member of an executive body (whether described as the board of directors or otherwise) of a body corporate as an employee of that body corporate in relation to those duties.

'Whether the director of a trustee company of a family trust is entitled to payment for performance of duties' will always ultimately be a question of fact in the particular circumstances.

Importantly, the actual payment for duties is not required, provided that the director is entitled to payment for performance of duties.

Where the director is an employee for these purposes, the deduction will only be available where three other conditions are satisfied. These are summarised below.

First, the member must be:

a an employee of the employer within the expanded meaning;
b engaged in producing the employer's assessable income; or
c an Australian resident who is engaged in the employer's business.

Secondly, one of the following requirements must be satisfied:

a the SMSF must be a complying superannuation fund;
b at the time the taxpayer made the contribution, the taxpayer had reasonable grounds to believe that the SMSF was a complying superannuation fund; or
c at or before the time the taxpayer made the contribution, the

taxpayer obtained a written statement (given by or on behalf of the SMSF) that the fund:

(i) was a resident regulated superannuation fund (within the meaning of the SIS Act); and

(ii) was not subject to a direction under the SIS Act, which prevents a fund from accepting employer contributions.

Finally, a deduction will only be available in the circumstances where the taxpayer made the contribution on or before the date that is 28 months after the end of the month in which the employee turns 75.

Payment of benefits

THE SMSF ESTABLISHED under most trust deeds (**Trust Deed**) is an allocated accumulation fund. This means the total amount of a member's accumulation account will be their entitlement in the fund on an access event.

The accumulation account is made up of all contributions, rollover payments and income on those amounts, less expenses and taxation.

Access events

Benefits are payable as either of, or a contribution of:

a a lump sum; or
b an income stream.

A number of rules apply to any income stream to be paid by the fund and specialist advice should be received before a member or beneficiary commences an income stream

The events which trigger access to benefits are:

a disability superannuation benefit—benefits are payable if a member has suffered physical or mental ill health and the member is unlikely to be gainfully employed again in a position for which the member is reasonably qualified due to their education, experience or training;
b retirement—once the preservation age is attained (explained below) a retirement following that date triggers access to benefits
c early retirement from employment—benefits can become payable on early retirement from employment;
d death—benefits must be paid on the death of a member; and
e TRIS—there can be access to a non commutable income stream upon attaining the relevant preservation age.

Preserved benefits

THE GOVERNMENT REQUIRES preservation of benefits until a member retires from the workforce on or after attaining the preservation age subject to exceptions such as total and permanent disablement or a TRIS.

The preservation age is 60, subject to the following exceptions:

Date of Birth	Preservation Age
After 30 June 1964	60
Between 30 June 1963 and 1 July 1964	59
Between 30 June 1962 and 1 July 1963	58
Between 30 June 1961 and 1 July 1962	57
Between 30 June 1960 and 1 July 1961	56
Before 1 July 1960	55

Generally, all benefits in a superannuation fund must be preserved until the member's preservation age. There are some limited exceptions to this rule, and again specialist advice should be sought before seeking to gain early access.

Death benefits

WHERE A MEMBER dies their benefit must be paid to:

a a superannuation dependant (essentially an immediate family member); or
b the member's LPR.

A beneficiary who is a superannuation dependant may also not qualify as a dependant for tax purposes (known as a 'tax dependant').

A tax dependant of deceased member includes only:

a any spouse;
b former spouse;
c any children under the age of 18; and
d any other person who was dependant upon or had an interdependency relationship with the deceased.

Tax will generally be payable on any benefits distributed other than to tax dependants.

The taxation consequences also differ depending on whether the amount is paid as a lump sum or an income stream and, in the case of an income stream, the ages of the deceased person and the recipient.

Only tax dependants can receive an income stream.

BDBNs

The trust deed permits BDBNs whereby a member can direct the trustee to pay their benefits on death to nominated dependants.

The BDBN can also specify the manner in which the member's

benefit is to be paid (that is lump sum or an income stream or both).

Advantages of BDBNs

Three of the main advantages of BDBNs are:

a reduced risk of successful disputes over death benefit payments;
b tax planning opportunities for member's with infant children; and
c asset protection planning.

Disadvantages of BDBNS

Three of the main disadvantages of BDBNs are:

a the tax and estate planning issues in relation to the payment of superannuation death benefits are complex and difficulties can often arise with BDBNs that prove to be inappropriate;
b if a member's circumstances change and they have failed to update their BDBN, the original BDBN will remain binding on the trustee; and
c a number of court decisions since 2012 have resulted in significant confusion about the exact requirements to ensure a BDBN is valid.

Members may also implement standard nominations (or non-BDBN), which give the trustee guidance as to where to pay a benefit, but need not be followed.

Taxation

Tax on payments

Benefits distributed to a member will be taxed either as a:

a Tax Free Component; or
b Taxable Component.

As the tax regime is complex, specialist advice should be sought, however broadly the position is as follows:

Lump sums	Age or dependant status	Tax treatment (Tax Rate %)	
		Tax Free Component	**Taxable Component**
Paid from a super fund	Under 55	0%	20%
	55 to 59	0%	Up to low rate threshold: 0% Balance: 15%
	60 and over	0%	0%
Death benefit	Tax dependant	0%	0%
	Non-tax dependant	0%	15%, or 30% on certain insured benefits
Pensions	**Age**		**Tax treatment**
Paid from super fund	55 to 59	0%	[Taxable component x marginal tax rate] –15% rebate
	60 and over	0%	0%

Death pension – reversionary pension paid to tax dependant (RB) of a primary beneficiary (PB) on death	PB < 60 and RB < 60	0%	[Taxable component x marginal tax rate] –15% rebate
	PB < 60 and RB > 60	0%	0%
	PB > 60	0%	0%

The low rate threshold is $195,000 for the 2015/2016 financial year. This amount is reduced by any amount previously applied to the low rate threshold.

Where benefits have not been subject to contributions tax in the fund (i.e. there is an element untaxed in the fund), an untaxed plan cap applies. This cap is set at $1,395,000 for the 2015/2016 financial year.

Rollovers

If a member's benefits are rolled over into another superannuation fund, approved deposit fund or annuity, no tax is payable until they ultimately receive the benefit.

Concessional contributions

Concessional contributions are sourced from pre-tax income. If a contribution is made within the concessional contribution limit it is taxable in the hands of the trustee at 15%. Any contributions above the concessional contribution limit trigger an additional tax of 31.5% on top of the 15%.

Non-concessional contributions

Non-concessional contributions are sourced from after tax income. Personal non concessional contributions within the non-concessional contribution limit are not subject to tax.

Non-concessional contributions above the non-concessional contribution limit are taxed at the top marginal rate of 46.5%, plus Medicare levy.

Low income spouse rebate

An income tax rebate of up to $540 per annum is available to a person who makes a superannuation contribution to a complying superannuation fund on behalf of a low or no income spouse under the age of 65 years.

To qualify for the rebate a number of conditions must be satisfied including:

a contributions must be from after tax income; and
b the spouse's assessable income must be less than $13,800.

Income tax

The standard tax rate for an SMSF is 15%.

The effective tax rate may be less than 15% due to imputation credits paid to an SMSF.

When franking rebates exceed the 15% rate, an SMSF can use the excess to offset its tax liability on other income.

An SMSF is also entitled to a refund of excess imputation credits if there is no other assessable income (and therefore no tax liability) to take advantage of the excess rebate.

However 'special' income is taxed at 46.5%. Special income includes:

a income where the fund and the other entity are not dealing with each other at arm's length; and

b. certain trust distributions (from discretionary or unit trusts) where the distributions are not at arm's length.

Deductions

General rules for deductions apply to SMSFs. This means that fund expenses are deductible to the extent to which they are incurred in gaining or producing assessable income.

Some expenses of an SMSF which are generally deductible include:

a. administration fees;
b. actuarial costs;
c. accountancy and audit fees;
d. costs of providing death or disability benefits such as insurance premiums; and
e. investment adviser fees.

CGT

A one-third discount applies on any capital gain an SMSF realises if the asset has been owned for more than 12 months.

Subject to strict rules, the small business CGT retirement exemption of $500,000 from the sale of an 'active business asset' by a member can be rolled into an SMSF.

GST

Generally the investment activities of an SMSF do not have GST consequences. However, certain transactions may constitute taxable supplies, in which case the SMSF must collect GST and remit it to the ATO.

One example relates to limited recourse borrowing arrangements (explained later in this book). In this regard the ATO's position is that the borrowing trust is in essence a bare trust of which the SMSF is the absolutely entitled beneficiary.

Therefore the ATO adopts a 'look through' approach in considering the relevant entity that is 'carrying on the enterprise.' The ATO recognises that in bare trust arrangements the beneficiary (that is the SMSF) is usually the entity making the ultimate supply or acquisition.

This means the SMSF in a borrowing trust arrangement is usually the entity that is required to be registered for GST given it is the entity that is 'carrying on the enterprise' for the purpose of acquiring the relevant enterprise.

Other information

Annual statement

The trustee should issue an annual statement to each member confirming their current entitlements in the fund.

Deed variation

The trust deed allows the trustee to vary the trust deed.

However, any variation cannot reduce the accrued benefits of a member without the consent of that member unless the reduction is required to enable the fund to continue to comply with legislative requirements.

Medical evidence

The trust deed allows the trustees to effect insurance for death and disability.

The insurance company that undertakes the insurance may require certain information about a member's medical condition before allowing the trustee to obtain a policy.

Expenses

Various expenses of operating an SMSF can be debited as the trustee determines against the members' accumulation accounts, including:

a the costs of any insurance policy or annuity;
b tax on contributions, investment earnings or other fund income or benefits payments;
c administrative expenses including the costs of preparing and lodging the annual ATO returns; and
d investment losses.

Forfeiture

The trust deed allows a member's benefits to be forfeited in certain circumstances, including:

a on an attempted assignment or charge of a benefit; and
b where in the opinion of the trustee any fraud, embezzlement or serious misconduct as a member have occurred.

Upon forfeiture, the entitlement can be dealt with as the trustee determines.

For obvious reasons, there are extremely strict provisions that must be followed before a member's entitlement can be forfeited and specialist advice should always be obtained.

Subject to certain criteria, a member's benefits are however protected from the claims of creditors in the event of bankruptcy or insolvency.

In particular, a member's entitlement in an SMSF, while they remain in accumulation mode, will generally be protected on bankruptcy, with no dollar limit to this level of protection.

Winding up funds

The trust deed allows for the fund to be wound up.

An SMSF can be wound up at any time.

Specialist advice should be obtained before winding up an SMSF, as there are a range of issues to be addressed including:

a taxation, stamp duty and other costs on the transfer of assets;
b complying with the trust deed;
c discharging all liabilities, outstanding tax and charges;
d preparation and lodgement of tax and regulatory returns and notifications; and
e potentially deregistering any corporate trustee.

Non compliance

If an SMSF is deemed by the ATO to be non-complying then the following taxation consequences generally arise:

a for every year that the SMSF remains non-complying, its assessable income is taxed at highest marginal tax rate;
b in the year that it becomes non-complying, it includes in its assessable income an amount equal to the market value of the SMSFs total assets (less any contributions the fund has received that are not part of the taxable income of the fund);
c the pension exemption is not available;
d a general interest charge is also usually payable, which can be significant where the ATO issues the notice of non-compliance in respect of a financial year from many years earlier.

The ATO has confirmed that it will consider the following factors when deciding whether to issue an SMSF with a notice of non-compliance:

a The tax consequences in making an SMSF non-complying and the financial impacts this would have on the members of the fund;
b The seriousness of the contravention, including:
   (i) trustee's behaviour;
   (ii) the effect the contravention has on the SMSF's assets; and
   (iii) the number and duration of contraventions.

c All other relevant circumstances, including:
   (i) if the trustee has rectified the contravention;
   (ii) the level of skill and knowledge of the trustee;
   (iii) the compliance history of the fund; and
   (iv) the events which led to the contravention.

Generally the ATO argues that its main focus is encouraging SMSF trustees to comply with the superannuation laws, and therefore it will prefer to utilise one of the following approaches, rather than make a fund non-complying:

a trustee education and direction;
b enforceable undertakings;
c rectification direction;
d administrative penalties;
e disqualification of a particular trustee (or director of a corporate trustee;
f civil and criminal penalties;
g allowing the SMSF to be wound up; and
h temporary freezing of an SMSF's assets.

Is the trust deed up to date?

DIFFICULTIES CAN ARISE if an SMSF trust deed is not up to date and compliant with the law and planning strategies.

Any deficiency in the trust deed could result in there being substantial extra tax to pay, a severe lack of flexibility and possibly certain trustee decisions being rendered invalid. In an estate-planning context, some of the issues that should be considered include whether:

a. the deed permits the making of a BDBN;
b. there are any restrictions in relation to BDBNs (assuming they are permitted)—for instance, whom they may be paid to, whether the benefit is to be paid as a lump sum or as a pension, or whether there are time limits within which the death benefit is to be paid;
c. the deed permits a broad range of benefit options, including lump sum benefits, pensions and a mixture of both. The deed should also authorise reversionary pensions – that is, allowing the member's pension to be paid to the member's dependants upon the member's death;
d. the deed complies with current legislative provisions;
e. the deed allows for individual and/or corporate trustees, as desired;
f. benefits can be paid out in kind;
g. in kind contributions can be made; and
h. eligible spouse contributions can be made.

Generally, in the absence of the need to be prescriptive in specific areas, SMSF trust deeds should be drafted so as to be as flexible as possible.

Age of trust deed

THE AGE OF the trust deed is generally a significant determinant of whether it should be updated. Specifically, there are some critical dates which, if the trust deed were established, or the most recent amendment occurred, prior to that date then serious consideration should be given as to whether the trust deed needs updating.

The superannuation system, as a whole, changed considerably with the introduction of the SIS Act. Generally speaking, trust deeds established prior to that date should be updated. SMSFs which still have trust deeds executed prior to that date raise additional concerns about how the fund obtained a notification that it is a complying fund – that is, a fund that complies with the provisions of the SIS Act and which requires an election by the fund trustee that the SIS Act applies to the SMSF.

Further significant amendments to the SIS Act were made in 2003 with, among other things, the introduction of the co-contribution rules.

Spouse contribution splitting was introduced on 1 January 2006 before the simplified super reforms came into force on 1 July 2007. The simplified super changes were arguably the most comprehensive changes since the introduction of the SIS Act and included:

a changes to the taxation of eligible termination payments;
b changes to the payment of death benefits;
c the abolition of reasonable benefit limits and the introduction of the contributions caps.

Deeds of variation

SUPERANNUATION TRUST DEEDS can be totally revoked and replaced with a completely new document, while changes to a family trust deed tend to be extremely piecemeal.

The issue can be largely answered by reference to the Tax Office's approach to resettlements.

Broadly, the Tax Office accepts that in relation to superannuation funds, a resettlement for tax purposes will never occur. Due to this approach (and stamp duty exemptions that apply in essentially every Australian state), most advisers recommend that when updating a superannuation trust deed, it is best to adopt a completely new deed.

In contrast, where updating a family trust deed, because of the risks associated from a resettlement perspective, it is usually best to only amend the provisions that are in particular need of being addressed.

Some SMSF trust deed providers offer an 'automatic update' online.

Specific advice should be obtained before adopting this approach as many SMSF specialists believe there are a number of significant risks, including:

a the updated trust deed could potentially be invalid as the automatic online process may not:
   (i) comply with the correct variation power or signing process;
   (ii) take into account if prior deeds have been properly executed;

b advisers involved in assisting with the obtaining of trust deeds online may also be engaged in legal practice and therefore in breach of the Legal Practice Acts of the relevant State/Territory;

c most professional bodies prohibit their members from preparing legal documents which should be carried out by lawyers;

d. advisers who are not practicing lawyers involved in this type of solution will generally be uninsured; and
e. these types of 'boilerplate' deeds often fail to address any complexity in the circumstances of the members, particularly in relation to estate planning, asset protection and BDBNs.

SMSFs and separate bank accounts

OFTEN WHERE AN SMSF trustee owns all of the units in a unit trust, if only from a cost perspective, the decision will be made to have one bank account—i.e. all of the monies that would otherwise pass to the unit trust and then ultimately be routed back to the SMSF pass directly to the SMSF.

The Tax Office has confirmed in an Interpretive Decision (ID 2014/7) that they believe such an approach breaches the superannuation legislation.

In particular, the Tax Office argues that the provisions of regulation 4.09A of the SIS Regulations require that an SMSF must keep its money and the other assets of the fund separate from any money or assets that are, for example, held by a trustee personally.

Practically however, where the SMSF maintains the bank account, they have arguably not breached regulation 4.09A, rather it may be the trustees of the unit trust that have failed to segregate the funds of the unit trust.

As unit trusts are not directly regulated by the superannuation laws, any breach of trust would have to be separately pursued, and where the trust is solely owned by the SMSF, it is unlikely that anyone would fact seek to complain.

Whether the Tax Office is likely to adopt such a pragmatic approach appears somewhat unlikely in the context of the interpretive decision mentioned above.

Similarly, in relation to borrowing trust arrangements, strictly speaking, a bank account should be opened in the name of the borrowing trust, the settlement sum for the trust would then be deposited into that bank account and the purchase price (having been advanced by the SMSF) would be paid from that account.

However, the ATO allows a 'look through' approach when dealing with these types of bare trusts which allows financial dealings to be in the name of the SMSF only, although legal title to the asset acquired must always be in the name of the borrowing trust.

Practically for borrowing trust arrangements this means:

a. The name on the purchase contract should be the trustee of the borrowing trust and ideally the contract should also name the trust (this will prevent any argument at a later date as to whether the trustee entered into the contract, and therefore owns the property, in its own capacity or as trustee of the borrowing trust).
b. Only one bank account, in the name of the SMSF, is necessary and that account can be used to bank the settlement sum for the borrowing trust, as well as conduct all transactions in respect of the asset. The trustee for the borrowing trust can direct any tenant to pay rental income directly to the SMSF's bank account and it does not have to be held in a separate bank account for the borrowing trust.
c. Similarly, all expenses of the asset can be also paid by the SMSF.
d. The purchase price of the asset can be recorded in the accounts of the SMSF – there is no need to prepare separate accounts for the borrowing trust.

Corporate trustees and SMSFs

WHILE THE INITIAL setup costs of a corporate trustee are generally higher than for individuals, there is a range of reasons why the use of a company is beneficial, including:

a the use of a corporate trustee provides limited liability protection. This can be particularly important if the SMSF owns real property;
b special purpose corporate trustees of an SMSF are entitled to discounted annual ASIC fees;
c in terms of what the auditor (and ultimately the Tax Office) expects to see, the use of a special purpose corporate trustee results in significantly improved record-keeping and compliance;
d from a succession planning perspective, it is significantly easier to regulate the control of a corporate trustee (by simply changing the directors from time to time) as opposed to that of individual trustees, where each time an individual trustee changes, there is often a mass of documentation to be prepared and notifications to be made; and
e in relation to sole member funds, the use of a corporate trustee significantly simplifies the overall structure of an SMSF, as a sole director company is permissible. In contrast, it is impossible to create a valid SMSF with an individual trustee and sole member because, in this instance, there must always be an additional individual who acts as a co-trustee.

Pensions and commutation

WHEN REVIEWING THE pension and commutation provisions of a deed, ideally the terms of a trust deed should be as flexible as possible and allow the payment of all types of pensions.

Some older deeds are particularly prescriptive in relation to the payment of pensions, this appears to have arisen on the basis that the SIS Regulations require that the rules for the payment of each type of pension ensure that certain prescribed conditions are met.

The prescriptive approach seems to have been adopted in older deeds as it was assumed that, if the rules for the payment of each type of pension were not set out clearly in the trust deed, and pensions were not paid in accordance with these rules, the requirement to ensure that pensions were paid in a particular way could not be met and the SIS Regulations would be contravened.

However, the governing rules of an SMSF include not only the terms of the trust deed but also any rules contained in other documentation and any unwritten rules.

Therefore, the more modern approach is to have the pension provisions in the trust deed drawn as flexibly as possible.

Reserves

IN RELATION TO reserve accounts, it is generally recommended that the trust deed provide for the creation of reserve accounts. This is particularly important in relation to excess contributions.

Re-contribution strategy

ANY SAVINGS (AND any earnings on these savings) held within superannuation that are 'tax-free components' are able to be distributed tax-free on death.

Tax-free components include:

a non-concessional contributions (formerly referred to as 'un-deducted contributions'), where no tax deduction has been received in relation to amounts contributed (for example, contributions made from post-tax earnings); and
b government co-contributions.

One strategy that was historically of benefit involved withdrawing the taxable component from superannuation and then re-contributing it as a non-concessional contribution, with the result that all benefits became tax-free and enabled the whole super benefit to be paid to non-dependants as a lump sum, tax-free on a member's death.

Since 1 July 2007, the usefulness of this strategy has been weakened because:

a any withdrawal from an SMSF on a lump sum basis must be made proportionately as between tax-free and taxable components. In other words, it is not possible to withdraw only the taxable component;
b there are significant limitations placed on the ability to contribute tax-free components to superannuation, namely:
   (i) non-concessional contributions are limited to $540,000 every three years, where the member is under 65 years of age;
   (ii) non-concessional contributions are limited to $180,000 per year where the member is over 65 years of age and the member satisfies the work test; and

(iii) no contributions can be made once the member reaches 75 years of age.

An alternative strategy that has developed is the establishment of an additional SMSF to receive all non-concessional contributions (tax-free components) so that, upon the member's death, the whole super benefit is paid to non-dependants, with the vast majority of that benefit being tax-free (although any earnings from investing the tax-free component are taxable). For example, the member could contribute any pension payments received or any after-tax amounts to the newly established SMSF.

Chapter Two

INVESTMENT BORROWING STRUCTURES

Overview

GENERALLY, THE TRUSTEE of an SMSF is prevented from borrowing money or maintaining an existing borrowing, unless the trustee complies with provisions of section 67A of the SIS Act.

It is important to note that, notwithstanding the borrowing might otherwise comply with the limited recourse borrowing provisions in section 67A of the SIS Act, there must be a specific power for the trustee to borrow, contained in the trust deed.

Furthermore, most financiers will require a number of other specific powers in the trust deed including:

a the power to grant the security for the borrowing;
b the power to instruct the trustee of the trust which is to hold the asset that is the subject of the borrowing;
c the ability for the SMSF trustee to be indemnified out of the assets of the SMSF, in the event the financier takes action;
d the ability to accept various types of contributions, which will be used by the SMSF trustee to make the repayments on the borrowing; and
e the power to grant a power of attorney to provide to the financier the ability to act on behalf of the fund, in the event of default.

Other than the limited recourse borrowing provisions in section 67A of the SIS Act, the main way an SMSF can potentially borrow is investing via a geared unit trust.

Limited recourse borrowing arrangements

In summary, a limited recourse borrowing trust structure ensures that:

a. any asset acquired by the borrowing trust is held by the trustee on trust for the SMSF;
b. the SMSF has the sole beneficial interest in all of the assets of the borrowing trust; and
c. the SMSF has a right, by making one or more payments to the lender (**Lender**), to acquire legal ownership of all of the assets in the borrowing trust.

Any investment by the SMSF should comply with the investment rules prescribed by the SIS Act and SIS Regulations (together referred to as the **Law**), in particular, sections 67A and 67B if it meets the following criteria:

a. the SMSF has borrowed money from the Lender which it has applied to acquire an original asset or a replacement asset (**Asset**) which the SMSF is permitted to acquire;
b. the rights of the Lender as against the SMSF are of a limited recourse nature against the SMSF's interest in the Asset; and
c. the Asset is the only asset held by the trustee of the limited recourse borrowing trust on trust for the SMSF.

Relevant investment rules

Prohibition on borrowings

Section 67(1) of the SIS Act contains a general prohibition against SMSFs borrowing, however, section 67A of the SIS Act allows borrowing in a narrow range of circumstances.

Limited recourse borrowing arrangements

An SMSF may borrow where the:

a money is used to acquire an Asset that the trustee is permitted under the law to acquire (**first requirement**);
b Asset is held on trust so that the trustee acquires a beneficial interest in the Asset (**second requirement**);
c trustee has a right to acquire legal ownership of the Asset by making one or more payments (**third requirement**);
d rights of the Lender (or any other person) against the trustee for default on the borrowing are limited to rights relating to the Asset (**fourth requirement**); and
e rights of the Lender (or any other person) against the trustee for the trustee's exercise of any rights it may have are limited to rights relating to the Asset (**fifth requirement**).

Further comments in relation to each of the above requirements are set out in turn below.

First requirement

The SMSF must ensure that any borrowing is applied for the acquisition of a single acquirable asset. The asset must be one which the SMSF is permitted under the Law to acquire.

Some examples of assets that an SMSF can acquire include:

a business real property (even if it is owned by a related party);
b listed shares (even if it is owned by a related party);
c residential property (although not if it is not owned by a related party); and
d a collection of assets that have the same market value and are identical to each other.

Advice should be obtained before an SMSF acquires an asset not listed above to ensure it is in accordance with the Law.

One example of the potential risks in this regard is where three lots of a property are to be acquired simultaneously. In this situation, if each of the three lots can be sold and dealt with separately, the ATO is likely to treat each lot as a distinct asset.

The fact that the property may be used as a single commercial space, even if there are no dividing walls, does not change this outcome.

In this type of situation it would therefore be necessary for three separate borrowing trusts to be established (that is, one for each lot), together with three separate loans to be made and, ideally, three separate contracts of sale.

This said, in some limited circumstances, the ATO accepts that property held on multiple titles can be a single acquirable asset (e.g. if a factory is built across a number of lots such that the lots cannot be used or dealt with separately).

In particular, the ATO in SMSFR 2012/1 confirms that where more than one real property lot is being acquired, the property will be a 'single acquirable asset' where there is a:

a unifying physical object, such as a permanent fixture which extends across two or more lots; or
b requirement at law that the lots are dealt with together, for instance where water rights attach to a particular lot.

There are some exceptions to this rule, such as where multiple identical assets are being acquired (e.g. 100 shares in a listed company).

Importantly however, the SIS Act does not prevent the acquisition of multiple lots of land. Rather, it prevents an SMSF from borrowing to acquire multiple lots (unless a separate trust is established for each lot).

SMSFR 2012/1 makes it clear that the relevant prohibitions apply to the asset that is acquired at settlement of the contract. For instance, in relation to the prohibition on an SMSF borrowing to improve an asset, the ATO gives the following example:

'*A similar outcome results if the contract is entered into for the purchase of a single title vacant block of land along with the constructions of a house on that land before settlement occurs. In this situation, the deposit paid upon entering into the contract and the balance payable upon settlement is applied for the acquisition, under that contract, of land with a completed house on it. The deposit and the balance payable at settlement may be funded under a single limited recourse borrowing arrangement.*'

Second requirement

The trustee of the borrowing trust will hold any asset on trust for the SMSF and the trust deed provides that the SMSF has a beneficial interest in each asset as the sole beneficiary.

Third requirement

The Trust Deed provides the SMSF with a right to acquire the legal ownership of any asset held via the limited recourse borrowing trust by making one or more payments.

Fourth requirement

The rights of the Lender (or any other person) against the SMSF trustee for default on the borrowing are usually contained in the loan establishment documents and must be limited to rights relating to the Asset, such that the Lender has limited recourse against the interest held by the SMSF.

Fifth requirement

If the SMSF has rights relating to the Asset (other than a right to acquire legal ownership by making one or more payments), the arrangements must be structured so that the rights of the Lender or any other person against the SMSF trustee for that trustee's exercise of its rights are limited to rights relating to the Asset.

Conclusion

If all five conditions are satisfied, then the SMSF can borrow from the Lender to acquire the Asset.

Borrowings

THERE ARE NO rules about who the Lender can be, such that the Lender can be the member, or a party related to the member.

The wider provisions of the Law continue to apply in relation to the SMSF trustee and its investment decisions, including that all arrangements must be at arm's length.

The loan between the SMSF trustee and the Lender must reflect market conditions for similar arrangements, including the interest rate, rate of repayment, any defaulting rate of interest and the term of the loan.

Prohibition on charging assets

GENERALLY, UNDER THE terms of loan documents, the Lender will take security over the Asset. Any security will represent a charge over the Asset which is held by the trustee of the borrowing trust on trust for the SMSF.

Generally, SMSFs are prohibited from giving a charge over or in relation to an asset of a fund under regulation 13.14 of the SIS Regulations.

However, regulation 13.15 permits a charge where it is otherwise permitted by the Law.

Where the loan documentation creates security over the Asset, it will be pursuant to section 67A of the SIS Act. Therefore, the exception to the prohibition against charging assets under regulation 13.15 applies to the Asset held on trust by the trustee of the limited recourse borrowing trust for the SMSF.

Prohibition on improving assets

SECTION 67A OF the SIS Act only permits a superannuation fund to borrow to:

a acquire an asset; or
b maintain or repair an existing asset.

In order to ensure compliance with the SIS Act, any improvements to an asset the subject to a borrowing arrangement would need to be funded using the SMSFs cash reserves, rather than borrowed funds.

In addition, care must be taken to ensure that any improvements to, for example, an existing building are not substantial enough to result in a fundamental change to the character of the original 'single acquirable asset'.

SMSFR 2012/1 gives the example of a residential house being built on vacant land changing the fundamental nature of the asset from vacant land to residential premises and therefore resulting in a different asset being held by the borrowing trust.

IHA rule

SECTION 71 OF the SIS Act imposes restrictions on the IHAs that can be owned or invested by an SMSF, or any related trust, generally to a maximum of 5% of the market value of the SMSF's assets.

However, section 71(8) of the SIS Act is an exception to the IHA rule. It provides that any investment in a related trust as part of a limited recourse borrowing arrangement that meets the requirements of the borrowing exception in section 67A is only an IHA under if the underlying asset would itself be an IHA of the SMSF if it were held directly.

This means that the investment by the SMSF in an arrangement that meets the requirements of sections 67A and 67B is not automatically counted against the 5% IHA limit.

Therefore, the IHA rules do not need to be considered where the arrangement otherwise meets the requirements of sections 67A and 67B, provided the asset which is the subject of the borrowing would not itself be an IHA.

A trustee of an SMSF intending on entering into a limited recourse borrowing arrangement should specifically ensure that:

a the SMSF obtains further legal advice if it intends to acquire an asset not clearly within the permitted investments for SMSFs; and
b any loan documentation limits the rights of the Lender (or any other person) against the SMSF trustee:
   (i) for default on the borrowing; or
   (ii) for the SMSF trustee's exercise of its rights relating to the Asset,
   (iii) to rights relating to the Asset as outlined above.

SMSF borrowing arrangements and business succession

WHERE MORE THAN one SMSF is involved with borrowing trust, the business succession arrangements should be carefully considered.

The main approaches, noting that the preferable solution depends on the exact commercial circumstances are as follows:

a As the intention with the borrowing arrangements is normally that they are self-funded, some clients choose to leave the structure in place and have an unfunded agreement (for example, a unit holder's agreement) regulating how the parties will conduct themselves if one of the principals passes away. In other words, the deceased's estate would treat the ownership interest in the building as an arm's length investment and would effectively maintain that interest until the other principal had sufficient funds to acquire the interest, or alternatively, the entire property was sold to a third party.

b Each principal can self-own insurance to pay out any debt referable to their interest in the underlying property. Having done this, the arrangement can then proceed essentially along the same lines as set out above.

c Each principal can obtain sufficient insurance to clear the entire debt. The buy-sell arrangement would require that 50% of the proceeds are paid to each principal (or their estate). The underlying property can then be dealt with as set out above, or alternatively, steps can also be taken to ensure that the property is transferred to the surviving principal's benefit, although the involvement of superannuation funds does create additional complications.

d. A final alternative where there is only one SMSF involved utilises cross owned insurance policies. In business succession arrangements, cross owned insurance policies are rarely, if ever, utilised. Avoiding the use of cross owned policies is driven by a range of commercial reasons and the fact that invariably adverse tax consequences are unnecessarily triggered as the desired commercial outcomes can normally be achieved utilising self-owned policies that almost always deliver favourable tax outcomes.

Where an SMSF has a limited recourse borrowing trust arrangement in place to acquire an asset which forms a substantial part of the total value of the fund, cross owned policies can be very useful.

An example of how this approach (which historically had been given in principle support by the Tax Office) can work is as follows:

a. The SMSF establishes a borrowing trust and borrows funds from a third party to acquire an asset.
b. The (say) only two members of an SMSF are concerned that on the death of one of them, the ability to pay out the member's entitlement may be impossible to achieve without selling the underlying asset (i.e. neither member's account balance is large enough to represent the entire value of the acquired asset).
c. If the members took out self-owned insurance policies, this would obviously not assist, given that the exiting member would effectively be entitled to an even greater share of the total assets of the fund.
d. In contrast, if permissible under the trust deed for the SMSF, if cross owned policies are implemented, then the remaining member's balance would be the one that increases and the cash from the insurance policy could be used to pay the death benefit, while the continuing member would effectively have their member balance represented entirely by the asset originally acquired via the borrowing trust.

How exactly this style of arrangement needs to be structured depends on the particular circumstances, however where appropriate, it can provide significant planning opportunities. Great care should however be taken with the approach as, despite strong criticism from many specialist advisers, the Tax Office is on record as saying this style of strategy is not permissible in its view.

Insurance funded business succession generally

For many years, the ownership of insurance policies for business succession buy-sell arrangements through an SMSF has been popular, at least anecdotally. A detailed analysis of business succession is outside the scope of this book, however the author has published a book titled 'The Seven Foundations of Business Succession'.

In broad terms, primary advantages of business succession insurance policy ownership via an SMSF include:

a the premiums in relation to the insurance policies are normally deductible, 'freeing up' money outside the superannuation environment that would otherwise be needed to fund insurance premiums;
b the insurance proceeds can often be utilised within the SMSF to generate tax effective income streams via pensions; and
c BDBNs (whether lapsing or non-lapsing) can be used to ensure that the proceeds from the policy pass as intended by the exiting partner.

In deciding whether or not to structure insurance ownership through an SMSF, there are numerous issues that need to be considered, including:

a the impact of contribution limits, which can significantly undermine the usefulness of the strategy in many situations;
b whether there are circumstances surrounding the structure, which might jeopardise the ability of the SMSF to satisfy the sole purpose test, set out under the SIS Act. The ATO has

publically flagged this as an issue, presumably where an SMSF has few, if any, other investment activities; and

c whether the arrangements are likely to fall foul of the general anti-avoidance provisions under part IVA of the Tax Act.

Historically the ATO has confirmed in various private documents that, when structured appropriately, an SMSF can own an insurance policy designed to assist the funding of a buy-sell arrangement, without breaching any tax or superannuation laws. In ATOID 2015/10 however the Tax Office confirmed its view that business succession insurance arrangements via an SMSF breach both the sole purpose test and financial assistance prohibition under the SIS Act.

It should also be remembered that there is the ongoing risk that some form of cap (not dissimilar to the former 'reasonable benefit limit' system) will be imposed on withdrawals from superannuation.

Example - Bank funding – limited recourse secured over property and other personal assets

The members of the SMSF offer their personal assets or act as a guarantor to provide additional security to the bank to secure the borrowing by the SMSF.

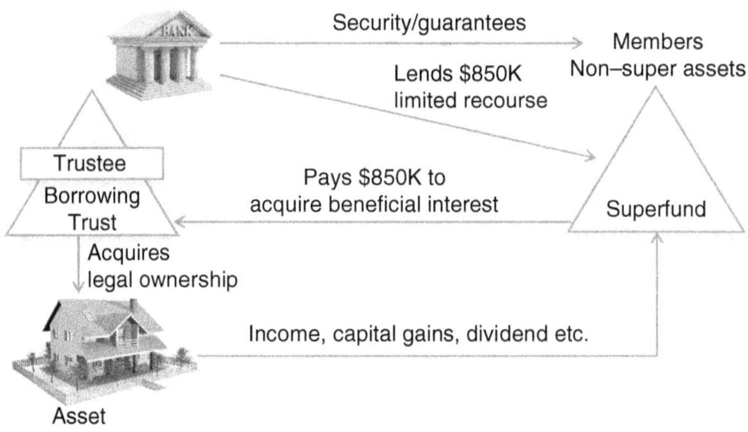

Bank funding – limited recourse secured over property

The SMSF is able to secure the borrowing from the bank without any member of the SMSF offering their personal assets or acting as a guarantor.

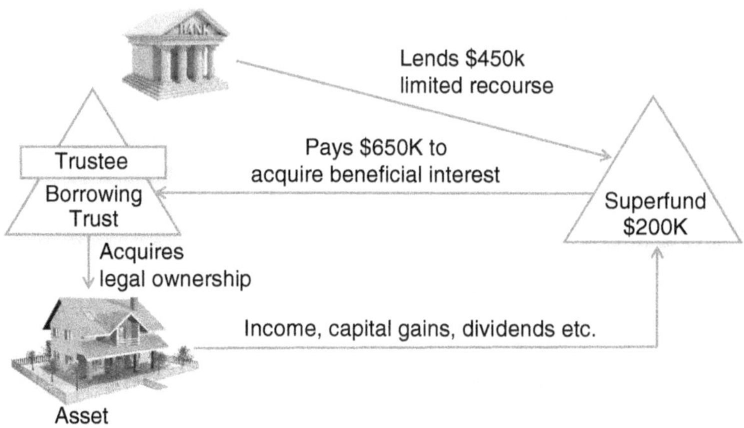

Self-funded – limited recourse secured over property

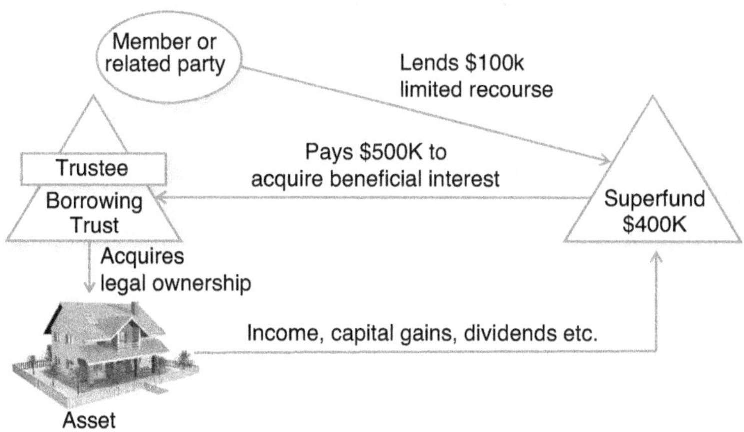

Geared Unit Trusts

WHERE A TRUST is not a 'related trust' under the SIS Act, then SMSFs can invest in it, even if the trust is geared, subject to certain rules, including:

a the trust deed for the SMSF permits the acquisition;
b the SMSF continues to comply with the SIS Act and SIS Regulations, particularly the sole purpose test; and
c the investment strategy for that SMSF justifies the basis on which the investment is made.

As set out below, generally an SMSF cannot invest in a related trust of the fund to an extent greater than 5% of the market value of the fund's total assets due to the IHA rules.

If an SMSF has IHAs with a value of more than 5% of the market value of the fund's total assets, then a range of penalties can be imposed by the ATO.

A geared trust should however not be a 'related trust' of an SMSF (and therefore not required to comply with the IHA rules) if it is structured so that:

a no one unitholder (including when grouped with 'related parties') can be entitled to more than 50% of the capital or income of the trust;
b no one unitholder (including when grouped with 'related parties') can control the trustee of the trust; or
c no one unitholder (including when grouped with 'related parties') can have the ability to unilaterally change the trustee of the trust.

Furthermore, any contractual arrangements between the unitholders (such as a unitholders agreement) must ensure that no aspect of the above prohibitions is breached.

Related parties

The SIS Act sets out who is a related party of an SMSF as follows:

a. a member of the fund;
b. a standard employer-sponsor of the fund; or
c. a 'Part 8 associate' of a member or standard employer-sponsor.

A 'standard employer-sponsor' is defined as being an employer who contributes to an SMSF.

A Part 8 associate of a member is defined as including:

a. their relatives;
b. other members of the SMSF and trustees or directors of the trustee of the SMSF;
c. the member's partners and partners' spouses or children ('partners' in this context refers to tax and general law partnerships, not life partners);
d. a trustee of a trust that the member or a member and their related parties control; and
e. a company that is sufficiently influenced by, or a majority voting interest is held by the member or a member and their related parties.

Best practice dictates that each aspect of the key tests must be reviewed carefully before a SMSF proceeds to invest in a geared unit trust.

Under section 70E (2) of the SIS Act, an entity will 'control' a trust if:

a. a group in relation to the entity has a fixed entitlement to more than 50% of the capital or income of the trust;
b. the trustee of the trust, or a majority of the trustees of the trust,

is accustomed to or under an obligation (formal or informal) or might reasonably be expected to act in accordance with directions, instructions or wishes of a group in relation to the entity (whether those directions, instructions or wishes are, or might reasonably be expected to be, communicated directly or through interposed companies, partnerships or trusts); or

c a group in relation to the entity is able to remove or appoint the trustee, or a majority of the trustees.

Section 70E (3) of the SIS Act defines a 'group' to mean:

a the entity acting alone;
b a Part 8 associate of the entity acting alone;
c the entity and one or more Part 8 associates of the entity acting together; or
d two or more Part 8 associates of the entity acting together.

What does 'sufficiently influenced' mean?

THE CONCEPT OF whether a director is 'sufficiently influenced' by other persons is always one of the most important issues that needs to be resolved before an SMSF proceeds with this style of arrangement.

Generally, a director will be considered to be sufficiently influenced by a third party where they act in accordance with that other party's directions or wishes.

While the concept is relatively easy to define, its application in any specific factual scenario will almost always depend on an interpretation of the circumstances.

Some examples of where a director has been held to be sufficiently influenced by another person includes:

a A husband and wife (who were the only directors of a company) have been held to be influenced by their sons, because they never made any substantive decision without consultation with the sons and their intention was to ultimately appoint the sons as directors.

b A company has been held to be controlled solely by one director, even when there was an independent third party as a co-director, because the third party had no input into the management of the company and had simply been appointed to create the impression that the board was independent.

c A sole director company, where the director was an independent appointment, was held to be controlled by the ultimate shareholders of the company, as the director simply acted in accordance with the directions of the shareholders.

Ultimately, the ATO has confirmed that it is necessary to take into account all of the evidence and conduct between parties and the concept of a party 'significantly influencing' a third party will exist where it can be said to be likely that the other party would act in accordance with the wishes expressed.

Section 71(4) - deemed IHA

EVEN WHERE THE technical provisions outlined above are satisfied, there is a potential risk that the ATO may review such an investment or arrangement and apply the 'catch-all' provision for IHAs contained in section 71(4) of the SIS Act.

Section 71(4) of the SIS Act extends the application of the IHA rule by providing that the ATO may determine that a loan or investment of an SMSF, or an asset subject to a lease or lease arrangement should be deemed to be an IHA even where it would otherwise fall outside the IHA tests in section 71 of the SIS Act.

Breach of IHA rules

IT SHOULD ALSO be noted that the IHA rules are subject to the civil penalty provisions under section 84(1) of the SIS Act and trustees of SMSFs may be subject to penalties where the rules are breached.

Specifically, a breach of the IHA rules will usually result in an SMSF losing complying fund status and entitlement to tax concessions.

However, a contravention of the IHA rules will not affect the validity of the transaction.

Example structure of a geared unit trust

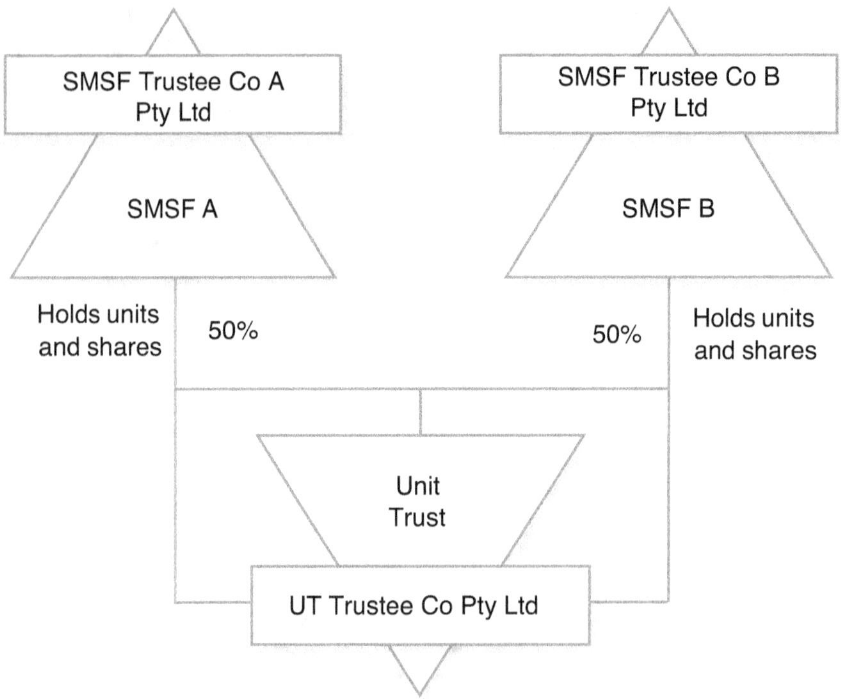

Public Trading Trust rules

A UNIT TRUST IS often an attractive investment vehicle for taxpayers, as it can offer many similar benefits to a corporate structure, with the following additional benefits not available to companies:

a access to the general CGT 33% discount (for SMSFs);
b the ability to issue units with different rights to income and capital;
c no requirements for formal disclosure to ASIC and other regulatory bodies; and
d no requirements for a formal audit.

Unit trusts are often viewed as the preferred structure for holding capital appreciating assets where there are unrelated third party investors.

Traditional unit trusts provide that the beneficial interest in the trust property is held in proportion to the units held by each unitholder.

It is important however to understand that under the Tax Act, a unit trust may be deemed (for tax purposes) to be a 'public trading trust'.

A unit trust may be held to be a public trading trust where one of more SMSFs hold a right to 20% or more of the income or capital of the trust and a number of other technical rules, explanation of which is outside the scope of this book, are satisfied.

Where a unit trust is deemed to be a public trading trust, the trust is in fact taxed as if it were a company, and all of the advantages outlined above will effectively be lost. For example:

a the trust's income (regardless of whether it is distributed or not) is taxed at the corporate tax rate;
b there may be insufficient franking credits for intended distribu-

tions due to (for example) depreciation rules;

c. if the trustee of the trust is unaware that it is in fact a public trading trust, it may be held to that all distributions are in fact unfranked dividends and cause significant excess tax to be paid;
d. there will be a delay for the SMSF in receipt of income, as the tax paid by the unit trust is refundable via a franking credit when the SMSF ultimately lodges its tax return.

Capital gains are taxed at the corporate tax rate, with no access to the CGT discount. This means for SMSFs in the accumulation phase, a tax rate of 15% rather than 10%.

IHAs

An SMSF may invest in a unit trust (subject to the application of the non-arm's length income provisions discussed below) provided that the unit trust is not a related party of the fund.

As noted earlier, there is a prohibition in the SIS Act which restricts the amount of IHAs that can be owned or invested by a SMSF to generally 5% of the market value of an SMSFs assets.

A unit trust that is controlled by a related party of an SMSF will be an IHA and caught by this prohibition, unless the trust satisfies the exemption in regulation 13.22C of the SIS Regulations (i.e. it is an ungeared unit trust).

With certain exclusions, an IHA of an SMSF is an asset that is any one of the following:

a. a loan to, or an investment in, a related party of the fund;
b. an investment in a related trust of the fund; or
c. an asset of the fund that is subject to a lease or lease arrangement between the trustee of the fund and a related party of the fund.

Generally, an SMSF cannot lend to, or invest in, a related party or related trust of the fund, where the loans, or the values of the assets that are the subject of the investment or lease arrangement, are greater than 5% of the market value of the fund's total assets.

If an SMSF has IHA with a value of more than 5% of the market value of the fund's total assets, then:

a the trustee may be disqualified
b the fund may be made non-complying
c a range of other penalties may be imposed (including prohibitions on acquiring further IHAs and prosecution).

Ungeared unit trusts

The test for whether a trust is controlled by a related party of an SMSF requires consideration of the fixed entitlements of the unitholders. In particular, a related party of an SMSF will be deemed to control the trust if the fund or its associates have a fixed entitlement to more than 50% of the capital or income of the trust.

There is an exception to the IHA test in SIS Regulation 13.22C for a unit trust that does not have any borrowings, notwithstanding that the trust may be a related party of an SMSF.

This commonly arises where an SMSF wishes to make an investment through a unit trust with other (non-superannuation fund) unitholders who can borrow to invest in the trust, or if no borrowing is required to fund the investment.

To be eligible for the exemption, the following conditions need to be met:

a the trust does not borrow;
b the trust does not invest in or loan money to individuals or other entities (other than deposits with authorised deposit-taking institutions);
c there is no charge over an asset of the trust;
d the trust has not acquired an asset from a related party of the fund other than business real property;
e the trust has not acquired an asset (apart from business real property) that had been owned by a related party of the fund in

the previous three years;

f the trust does not directly or indirectly lease assets to related parties other than business real property;

g the trust does not conduct a business; and

h the trust conducts all transactions on an arm's length basis.

Prior to 12 August 1999, an investment by a superannuation fund in a related unit trust was not an IHA. The transitional arrangements following the expansion of the definition of an IHA permit a fund to maintain an investment in a pre-12 August 1999 unit trust where the investment was not previously an IHA.

However, it is relevant to also bear in mind that the sole purpose test and the non-arm's length income provisions may still apply to the investment. Following 30 June 2009, any further investments in a pre-1999 unit trust will be an IHA unless a specific exemption applies.

Non-arm's length income

Income derived by an SMSF as a beneficiary of a trust, other than because of holding a fixed entitlement to the income, is non-arm's length income of the entity and will be taxed at penalty rates under the non-arm's length income provisions of the Tax Act. It is therefore important to ensure that the unit trust is a fixed trust for taxation purposes if the unitholder is an SMSF.

Income derived by a superannuation fund as a beneficiary of a fixed trust will also be non-arm's length income if:

a the fund acquired the entitlement under a scheme, or the income was derived under a scheme, the parties to which were not dealing with each other at arm's length; and

b the amount of the income is more than the amount that the fund might have been expected to derive if those parties had been dealing at arm's length.

To avoid the impact of the non-arm's length income rules, it is therefore vital for SMSFs to ensure that:

a no distributions are made to an SMSF from a discretionary trust; and
b where an SMSF owns units in a unit trust, that the unit trust is a fixed trust for tax purposes.

The ATO has expressed the view that the meaning of a 'fixed trust' must be ascertained from the terms of the relevant trust deed.

It is also relevant to note that the non-arm's length income rules may apply where an SMSF allows its fixed entitlement to remain as an unpaid present entitlement, as this generally does not reflect an arm's length arrangement.

When allowing unpaid present trust entitlements in favour of an SMSF, it is therefore necessary to ensure that interest on those unpaid distributions is paid by the trust at market rates as would be the case if the SMSF and trust were dealing with each other at arm's length.

Whether a unit trust is in fact a fixed trust is an area that has been the subject of significant uncertainty. Broadly it seems to be accepted that the following factors will be relevant to supporting that a trust is a fixed trust:

a the trustee cannot create different rights or different classes of units;
b all units on issue must have the same rights to receive income and capital of the trust;
c units must be allotted for market value;
d all income and capital of the trust must be distributed in proportion to the unitholdings, i.e. there is no discretion held by the trustee;
e partly paid units cannot be issued;
f the trust deed requires all unitholders to agree on the redemption of units and any redemption must be at market value;
g all valuations of the trust fund, and in turn the determination of unit values, must be conducted by a valuer in accordance with 'applicable Australian accounting principles';
h the trustee cannot make gifts; and

- the unanimous consent of all unitholders is required to vary the trust deed and the variation power should prohibit amendments to any of the above provisions.

Anti-avoidance rules

Finally in relation to investment structures for SMSFs, it is important to note that when taxation issues are considered as part of deciding how best to implement a specific transaction or wider arrangement, there is a risk that the ATO might review the transaction or arrangement and apply the general anti-avoidance rules contained in part IVA of the Tax Act.

Very broadly, part IVA may apply to the superannuation arrangements summarised above where it can be objectively determined from all the circumstances that the dominant purpose of any party to the transaction or arrangement, or to a part of the transaction or arrangement (**Scheme**), is to obtain a tax benefit for that party or another party associated with the Scheme.

The ATO must make a specific determination that part IVA applies. The ATO can then cancel the tax benefits otherwise obtained, reconstruct the transaction or arrangement for tax purposes and issue assessments, including penalties and interest relating to the disallowed tax benefit.

The interpretation of part IVA is highly technical and its application in each case requires a detailed consideration of the current case law and all the relevant facts. Furthermore, unless a binding ruling under part IVA is obtained from the ATO, it is not possible to provide certainty about its possible application.

Chapter Three

ESTATE PLANNING AND ASSET PROTECTION

Overview

Superannuation is often an individual's single most significant asset upon their retirements and potentially at the time of death.

The policies of several successive federal governments to encourage wealth accumulation via superannuation have resulted in a boom in retirement savings.

Despite the increase in wealth being held in superannuation, the estate planning steps necessary to ensure that an individual's entitlements pass as intended upon their death are commonly misunderstood.

The impact of these misunderstandings can be exacerbated when insurance is held in the superannuation environment, increasing the value of the wealth needing to ultimately pass to a beneficiary.

It is therefore important to have a comprehensive estate plan in place which addresses both estate and non-estate assets, particularly for SMSFs.

Proper planning can also reduce the likelihood that, after death, the recipients of superannuation benefits (and other assets) will have to pay unnecessary tax or find those assets exposed to unexpected risks.

The role of the trustee

In administering an SMSF, a trustee is normally given a number of discretionary powers.

It is generally up to the trustee to determine whether a person's superannuation benefits are paid to a dependant directly or to their estate. If a trustee pays superannuation death benefits directly to a person's dependants, then the estate is bypassed.

If however superannuation benefits are distributed to the estate of the former member then they will be dealt with by the member's will (or the intestacy rules if there is no valid will).

Benefits paid via an estate can in turn be distributed to, for example, a testamentary trust set up under the former member's will. Testamentary trusts are outside the scope of this book, however the author has published a book titled 'The Seven Key Aspects of Testamentary Trusts'.

The trustee of an SMSF may also have the discretion to determine the form the death benefits are paid – that is either as a lump sum or income stream, or possibly a combination of both. Importantly however, if a benefit is to be paid from an SMSF to an estate it can only be paid in the form of a lump sum.

Broadly, the exercise of discretion by a trustee of SMSF, for example, when determining how to pay a death benefit where a non-BDBN has been made is not subject to review by the court unless one of the following three factors is present:

a. The trustee does not act in good faith;
b. The trustee does not give real and genuine consideration to the exercise of the discretion and the purposes for which the discretion was granted; or
c. Reasons for the decision are provided by the trustee, but those reasons are unsound.

Trusteeship issues within an SMSF

The trusteeship of an SMSF is governed by section 17A of the SIS Act.

The trustee may be either:

a. a company operating as a corporate trustee, with each member of the SMSF being a director of the company; or
b. more than one individual trustee, again with each member being a trustee.

An additional consideration when appointing trustees is that generally a person who is not a member of the SMSF is not permitted to be a trustee (or director of a corporate trustee). Single member funds are an exception to this rule as an SMSF is not permitted to have a sole individual trustee.

Consequently, a single member fund can appoint a second trustee.

Similarly, single member SMSFs can have a corporate trustee with two directors, with the second director being someone other than the member (although a single member fund can also have a company with the member as sole director).

The rules in relation to trusteeship obviously significantly impact on the control of an SMSF following the incapacity or death of a member.

Incapacity

Special rules apply where a member of an SMSF is incapacitated, in which case their legal personal representative (typically their attorney, pursuant to an enduring power of attorney) is permitted to act in that member's place as a trustee or director.

However the SIS Act merely authorises the appointment from a superannuation compliance perspective and does not set out the legal process by which the appointment can occur.

An analysis is therefore required of the relevant instrument (the trust deed or company constitution) and legislation (the Trusts Acts in each state or the Corporations Act).

If the SMSF has a corporate trustee, the attorney will usually need to rely on either:

a a resolution by the other directors appointing them as a director, pursuant to a rule in the company's constitution; or
b a resolution by the shareholders appointing them as a director, pursuant to the Corporations Act.

This process can obviously raise a number of issues where the incapacitated individual was the sole director or a majority shareholder of the company.

Similarly, if the SMSF has individual trustees, the attorney will usually be reliant on the remaining co-trustees passing a resolution pursuant to the deed to make the appointment.

Practically, the only way in which an attorney under an enduring power of attorney could act in the role as trustee for an SMSF would be for the existing member to be removed from their role as trustee or director of the corporate trustee, and for the attorney under that member's enduring power of attorney to be appointed as the new trustee or director in place of the member.

Importantly, the person seeking to become a trustee or director needs to be appointed under an enduring power of attorney of the member who is seeking to be replaced. A general power of attorney will not be sufficient.

If, in time, a member no longer requires the attorney to be the trustee/director, the attorney would resign as trustee/director and the member would be re-appointed as trustee/director.

Alternatively, if the SMSF trustee:

a is an individual, the SMSF trust deed should provide the members with the power to remove and appoint a trustee either personally or through a 'principal' style role (if applicable). If the power to remove and appoint is left with the trustee for the time being (that is, the attorney) that may cause the members difficulty if the attorney refuses to resign; or

b is a company, the constitution for the SMSF trustee should ideally give any fund members who are shareholders power to remove and appoint a director of the company.

Death

Upon the death of a member, steps must be taken to ensure the trusteeship of the SMSF continues to comply with the requirements above.

Individual trustees

As a starting point assets of an SMSF must be held in the trustee's name.

With individual trustees, this will require the transferring of the titles to all assets to the new trustee when a new member is admitted to an SMSF and in turn removing a trustee's name when a member leaves a fund upon death, retirement due to incapacity or otherwise.

This administrative burden can be time-consuming and costly.

The nomination of successor trustees is important when an SMSF has individuals as trustees. Some SMSFs have a 'founder' or 'principal' role vested in someone other than the members. This can be a powerful role as such a person will generally have the power to appoint or remove a trustee or vary the trust deed.

Without such a role, any remaining trustee/s, or if there are no trustees remaining, the LPR of the last remaining trustee has the power to appoint the new trustee.

Corporate trustees

When members are admitted to, or cease membership of an SMSF with a corporate trustee all that is required is that the person becomes, or ceases to be, a director of the company.

A notification of this change must be sent to the ASIC within 14 days of the change, although generally of time will be provided where a failure to comply with the 14 day period is due to the death of the director.

As the legal title to all the assets remains vested in the company (which continues to act as trustee), a corporate trustee of an SMSF can save considerable time and effort.

The main disadvantages of having a corporate trustee of an SMSF are the:

a upfront cost of establishing the trustee company;
b extra documentation required when establishing the SMSF; and
c ongoing annual fee payable to ASIC, although where the company is a 'special purpose' company and has as its sole activity acting as trustee of an SMSF, a discounted annual fee of around 25% of the normal annual fee is payable to ASIC.

Conversely, the main advantage of appointing individual trustees is that it is quick, simple and initially inexpensive. There are no establishment costs, less ongoing fees and less initial paper work required when setting up the SMSF.

For completeness it is noted that a corporate trustee of a borrowing trust does not satisfy the definition of 'special purpose company', despite the fact that an SMSF will be the sole beneficiary and the trust is therefore essentially part of the superannuation structure.

This is because a special purpose company only includes:

> *'a company….. if the sole purpose of the company is to act as the trustee of a regulated superannuation fund within the meaning of the SIS Act.'*

If the deceased member is a shareholder in the corporate trustee of an SMSF, it is important to specify the recipient of those shares in their will.

The Corporations Act gives shareholders voting rights and allows them to vote out directors of the company (subject to any provision to the contrary in the constitution of the corporate trustee).

Shareholders thus hold a considerable amount of power and care must be taken to ensure that appropriate beneficiaries of the shares are chosen and included in the will.

The beneficiaries holding the shares will often have the responsibility of appointing a new director of the trustee company of the SMSF.

The new director would, in turn, along with any other directors of the company, exercise discretion in paying death benefits, unless a valid BDBN has been made.

The powers of a person who receives the shares in the corporate trustee of an SMSF are subject to at least two possible limitations, namely:

a any 'founder' or 'principal' role under the SMSF trust deed vested in someone other than the shareholders of the trustee company (as mentioned above); or

b prohibitions set out in the constitution of the trustee company around the rights attaching to the shares. For example, the shares of a member may be automatically redeemed on the death of the member, or the voting rights attaching to the shares may be limited to a percentage equal to the proportionate share of the relevant members' member balance in the SMSF.

Income stream overview

A SUPERANNUATION DEATH BENEFIT may only be paid as an income stream to a 'dependant' of the deceased member.

If an income stream superannuation death benefit is paid to a child, then the income stream must be converted to a lump sum superannuation death benefit once the child reaches the age of 25. The decision to pay an income stream to a child needs to take this into account, especially if there is likely to be a large lump sum passing to the child at age 25.

Where a member has reached preservation age, and is already receiving their superannuation benefit as an income stream prior to death, it is possible to nominate a reversionary beneficiary for their benefit to ensure that, upon the member's death, the income stream is paid to their nominated beneficiary.

The tax treatment of both lump sum and income stream superannuation death benefits depends upon a number of factors and is explained below.

Ultimately, the trust deed governing a superannuation fund (together with any valid nominations) will determine the process for dealing with a person's superannuation assets upon their death.

Estate Planning Costs Paid Through an SMSF

In order to obtain the concessional taxation available for superannuation savings, an SMSF must have its sole purpose as being the provision of benefits to members on retirement, or their dependants or LPR on death.

In this context, one issue that is often raised is whether an SMSF can pay the costs of ensuring its members have their estate planning affairs in order.

In the absence of any specific guidance from the ATO in this area, there are a range of views about the legitimacy of this approach.

Some advisers believe that any estate planning related expense is clearly incurred in order to help provide for the dependants or LPR of a member and therefore properly payable by an SMSF.

The conservative position is that either all estate planning costs should be incurred by members personally, or alternatively where they may be paid by the SMSF, there must be a direct and clear nexus between the expense incurred and the ultimate provision of benefits to dependants or LPR on the death of a member.

While the conservative approach seems to be that all estate planning costs should be incurred by members personally, practically, there are a number of examples where having an SMSF incur the relevant expense would appear reasonably arguable, including:

a where an SMSF trust deed is being updated as part of an estate planning exercise, clearly these costs should be incurred by the fund;
b where, as part of the update, BDBNs are prepared (either on a standalone basis or 'hardwired' into the trust deed of the SMSF), then again these costs are legitimately payable by the fund;

c. where superannuation makes up a significant component of a member's overall wealth and the member intends (either via binding or non-BDBNs) for their superannuation entitlements to pass via their will, then the costs of the will (including any testamentary trusts incorporated into the documentation) should also be able to be paid by the SMSF;
d. strategic advice to members in relation to the impact of death on their superannuation entitlements should also be properly payable by the SMSF; and
e. while the nexus might be slightly less obvious, ensuring that a member has a legal personal representative able to take over the trusteeship of an SMSF may also justify a fund incurring costs for implementing a member's enduring power of attorney.

As with many similar topics, the general position outlined above will depend on the particular factual situation.

For completeness it is noted that part of the confusion with the rules in this area, particularly for financial advisers and risk advisers, undoubtedly is because of the relatively vague standards that most licensees seem to impose.

Some licensee rules provided that advisers can charge an SMSF for all advice that was either product related or strategically relevant to the SMSF.

In turn, often the rules will state that charging the SMSF for any other advice that is not so 'related' will potentially breach the sole purpose test and is therefore prohibited.

Unfortunately, the vagueness of the rules under this type of approach can make it difficult for advisers and clients alike to make decisions in relation to areas such as binding death benefit nominations and wider estate planning documentation, and until there is clearer guidance from, for example, the ATO, there is likely to be continuing uncertainty.

Deductibility of SMSF expenses

As a general rule, deductibility of expenditure incurred by an SMSF is determined under section 8-1 of the Tax Act, unless:

a a specific deduction provision in the Tax Act applies; or
b a provision of the Tax Act makes the expenditure specifically non-deductible.

To be deductible under section 8-1, the expenditure must not be a loss or outgoing of capital, or of a capital nature, or of a private or domestic nature.

Broadly, the following types of expenses typically incurred by an SMSF are deductible under section 8-1:

a costs of complying with the SIS Act, unless the cost is a capital expense;
b costs in connection with the calculation and payment of benefits to members;
c investment adviser fees and costs in providing pre-retirement services to members;
d other administration costs incurred in managing the SMSF;
e costs for advice where provided by a qualified lawyer.

Refreshing of cost base

AFTER DEATH, IN addition to any taxes triggered on the payment of funds or distribution of assets to dependants, an SMSF itself also must pay tax, at a rate of 10%, on the difference between the cost base and market value of each asset the subject of payment at the date of death.

As any sale of a capital asset prior to death (assuming the SMSF is in pension mode) is tax-free, one strategy often adopted is to actively 'refresh' the cost base of the assets in the SMSF. This is achieved by the following steps:

a assets with large capital gains are regularly sold and then reacquired, or other assets are acquired;
b the sale and reacquisition ensure that the cost base of the asset, for the SMSF, is regularly uplifted; and
c on death, the likely capital gain in relation to any particular asset is therefore minimised.

This approach needs to be managed carefully to ensure the anti-avoidance provisions of the Tax Act are not enlivened.

Accessing disablement proceeds via superannuation

Best practice often dictates that SMSF members should obtain insurance protection on the basis of an inability to work in their 'own', as opposed to 'any' occupation.

The satisfaction of the 'own' occupation test is obviously easier than the condition of release set out under the superannuation legislation, being that a member must be incapable of working in 'any' occupation.

Where insurance is owned via a superannuation fund there is therefore a risk that while the fund will receive an insurance payout, it will be unable to release it to the member until some other condition of release is satisfied (for example, reaching the retirement age).

Historically therefore, the conservative view was undoubtedly that own occupation insurance should always be owned outside super. Importantly, since 1 July 2014, own occupation insurance is no longer available via superannuation, subject to a grandfathering for arrangements already in place before that date.

For those pre-existing arrangements, there appears to be a pragmatic approach adopted, particularly by those with policies via an SMSF. This approach involves assuming that a trustee (who will also be a member of the relevant fund) will adopt a liberal interpretation of the 'any' occupation definition under the superannuation legislation and therefore always allow the release of insurance proceeds.

SMSFs and asset protection

Movement into bankruptcy

A lot must happen before a trustee in bankruptcy becomes involved.

In particular, there must be a debt.

If that debt is a judgment debt, there will have been a claim that has been successfully prosecuted in the courts.

There must then have been a failure to meet that debt.

The creditor must then have sought to appoint a trustee in bankruptcy to the debtor's estate.

Depending on the circumstances, other arrangements might be considered in order to avoid the appointment of a trustee in bankruptcy. The debtor might consider entering into an informal agreement with creditors, or entering into arrangements under parts IX or X of the Bankruptcy Act.

A discussion of these various arrangements and options is outside the scope of this book.

'Claw back' rules

In considering claims that might be brought by a trustee in bankruptcy, it is relevant to bear in mind the voidable transaction provisions in the Bankruptcy Act. These provisions, often referred to as 'claw back' provisions, enable the trustee in bankruptcy to trace and reclaim assets that were transferred prior to a person becoming bankrupt.

In particular, a transfer can be overturned, subject to certain exclusions:

a if the transfer took place within four years before the commencement of the bankruptcy where no consideration was paid or where consideration was less than market value; or
b if the transfer at any time before the commencement of the bankruptcy and at the time of the transfer the person was insol-

vent, where no consideration was paid or where consideration was less than market value; or

c if the transfer took place within six months before the commencement of the bankruptcy, the transfer is to a creditor, the creditor obtains a preference, priority or advantage over other creditors and at the time of the transfer the transferor was insolvent; or

d at any time where the main purpose in making the transfer is to prevent the transferred property from becoming divisible, or to hinder or to delay the process of making property available for division, among creditors.

It should be remembered that, as the commencement of the bankruptcy may be dated from the first act of bankruptcy within the six months before a relevant petition was presented, up to a further six months could be added to these periods of 'claw back'.

Companies and trusts

Similar provisions to those found in the Bankruptcy Act regarding voidable preferences are in the Corporations Act. Under section 588FE of the Bankruptcy Act the following transactions are voidable:

a an insolvent transaction within six months of the commencement of winding up of the company;

b an insolvent and uncommercial transaction within two years of the commencement of winding up;

c an insolvent transaction with a related party entered into within four years of the commencement of winding up; and

d an insolvent transaction which the company entered into for the purpose of defeating or delaying creditors – within ten years of the commencement of winding up.

The same rules apply to trusts depending whether the trustee is an individual or company.

Superannuation and bankruptcy

Legislative provisions

Historically the Bankruptcy Act provided that all property that belonged to a bankrupt at the start of a bankruptcy was divisible amongst the creditors of the bankrupt. Property was defined to exclude interest in a superannuation fund if certain qualifications were met. This meant that this protection of superannuation was not absolute.

From 1 July 2007 however assets held via a superannuation fund can only be 'clawed back' if the main purpose of the transferor was either to:

a prevent the transferred property being available to creditors; or
b hinder or delay the process of making property available for division among creditors.

To determine the main purpose for making the contribution it is presumed to be an attempt to defeat creditors if it can reasonably be inferred from all the circumstances that at the time of the transfer the transferor was, or was about to become, insolvent.

If insolvency is not an issue at the time of transfer, both sections provide that when determining the transferor's main purpose for making the transfer, regard must be had to whether the transferor had established any pattern of making contributions to one or more superannuation funds and if so whether the transfer under examination is out of character.

Therefore, as an example, contributions are unlikely to be made with the intention of defeating creditors if contributions have been made every year for the past 5-10 years.

However, it is debateable (as another example) if a contribution will be sufficiently 'unusual' to be for the purpose of defeating creditors if a person makes contributions utilising the accelerated non-concessional regime, profiled elsewhere in this book. This is despite the fact that such contributions are at law only able to be made in sporadic instalments.

Payments from superannuation

Generally lump sum payments from an SMSF to a bankrupt are protected from a trustee in bankruptcy, including if received on or after the date of bankruptcy.

Counterintuitively however, while specialist advice should always be obtained, it is often preferable to ensure no payments are received from superannuation until after a bankruptcy arrangement is entered into. This is because if payments are received by a member before bankruptcy the source of the funds may become merged or intermingled with other assets and no longer protected.

Anecdotally, there are situations where a trustee in bankruptcy has deliberately delayed a bankruptcy petition until after a member satisfies a condition of compulsory cashing in order to increase the prospects of a bankrupt's superannuation savings being available.

Similarly, the balance of a member's entitlements where they are in pension phase is generally protected. The income received by a member from pension payments are however assessed as income in the hands of the bankrupt.

This is important because under the Bankruptcy Act there are restrictions on how much income a bankrupt can earn before a proportion of the income is forfeited.

The formula used to determine the quantum of income that is paid to a trustee in bankruptcy is:

$$\frac{\text{Assessed income, less the income threshold}}{2}$$

'Assessed income' is essentially a bankrupt's gross income, less all tax (including Medicare).

The income threshold for a bankrupt is determined with reference to their dependants and is indexed regularly.

Notional estate provisions

A WIDER ASSET PROTECTION issue in relation to SMSFs and estate planning relates to the notional estate provisions that currently only apply in New South Wales.

Laws in each state of Australia allow a family member or certain other dependants to challenge a deceased's will. Such a claim is generally known as either a family provision application or a TFM claim.

Whether a TFM claim is successful, depends upon a range of matters – regardless of the outcome, however, TFMs can be costly and emotionally debilitating for all parties involved.

Historically in all Australian states, a TFM claim could only relate to property that was owned by the deceased on the date of their death, putting certain property such as SMSF assets, trust assets or those owned by a will maker's spouse outside the reach of a TFM claim.

In New South Wales however, special rules allow the courts to make orders in relation to assets that do not in fact form part of a deceased's personal estate.

In many respects, the rules are analogous to those under the Bankruptcy Act in that will makers who take steps to remove assets from their personal name leave those assets exposed to be 'clawed back' into the estate for the purposes of family provision applications made within 3 years of the date of their death.

While the rules apply to anyone living in New South Wales at the date of death, they also potentially apply where the will maker has any assets connected with New South Wales. This means that, in relation to SMSFs, the following situations may be exposed:

a. If there is one asset in the SMSF that has the necessary connection with New South Wales (e.g. a house), that may be sufficient to drag all assets of the SMSF into the New South Wales notional estate provisions.

b A company that is listed on the stock exchange, but happens to have its registered office in New South Wales, can be an asset that can be subject to the notional estate provisions automatically. Thus, even if an SMSF has no assets in New South Wales at all, but happens to own shares in a listed company that is registered in New South Wales, those shares are subject to the notional estate rules and again, all the other assets in the super fund are similarly exposed.

c Finally, if the trustee company of an SMSF is registered in New South Wales, even though the fund itself has no assets in New South Wales, this is sufficient to allow the New South Wales notional estate provisions to apply.

While there have to date been very few cases that have applied the notional estate provisions, each of the above possibilities should be taken into account by any member of an SMSF who is concerned that there estate planning arrangements may be challenged.

Chapter Four

DEATH BENEFITS

Overview

A SUPERANNUATION DEATH BENEFIT is a payment received from an SMSF because of the death of a person who was a member of that fund.

Death benefits do not automatically form part of a person's estate.

Rather, an analysis of the legislation, the SMSFs trust deed, relevant case law and in some instances, the manner in which the fund is controlled, need to be considered to determine how the superannuation death benefits should be paid.

Eligible recipients

Under section 62 of the SIS Act, a death benefit can only be paid to:

a a 'dependant' of the person; or
b the member's LPR, being the executors or administrators of their estate.

Dependants

The definition of 'dependant' is contained in section 10 of the SIS Act and includes:

a the spouse of the person;
b any child of the person; and
c any person with whom the person has an 'interdependency' relationship.

Under section 10A of the SIS Act, two persons have an interdependency relationship if:

a they have a close personal relationship;
b they live together;

c. one or each of them provides the other with financial support; and
d. one or each of them provides the other with domestic support and personal care.

Two people may also have an interdependency relationship if they have a close personal relationship and the only reason they fail to satisfy all the conditions in section 10A of the SIS Act is that either or both of them suffer from a physical, intellectual or psychiatric disability.

There are a range of factors that may or may not be taken into account when determining whether an interdependency relationship exists, some of which are:

a. the duration of the relationship;
b. whether or not a sexual relationship exists;
c. the ownership, use and acquisition of property;
d. degree of mutual commitment to a shared life;
e. care and support for children;
f. the reputation and public aspects of the relationship;
g. the degree of emotional support;
h. the extent to which the relationship is one of mere convenience; and
i. any evidence suggesting that the parties intend the relationship to be permanent.

The definition of 'dependant' also takes on its ordinary meaning and whilst there have been efforts in other contexts to give a very wide meaning to the term (for instance, to include emotional dependency), case law to date indicates that dependency in the superannuation context requires a degree of financial dependency.

The definition of dependant does not include grandchildren, unless the grandchild is financially dependent on the grandparent at the time of their death, or the member and the grandchild were in an interdependency relationship.

Therefore, generally a person cannot leave death benefits from their superannuation fund directly to a grandchild, however (as discussed in more detail below), they may pass the benefits to grandchildren or other non-dependants by nominating their LPR as the death benefit beneficiary and including specific gifts of the entitlements in their will.

Generally, children will not be in an interdependency relationship with their parents, however it may exist where:

a they have a close personal relationship, they live together and one or each of them provides the other with financial support; and
b one or each of them provides the other with support and care of a type and quality normally provided in a close personal relationship, rather than by a friend or flatmate.

Definition of LPR

LPR is defined in the SIS Act to include:

a the executor of the will;
b an administrator of the estate of a deceased person;
c the trustee of the estate of a person under a legal disability; and
d a person who holds an enduring power of attorney granted by a person.

LPR's are bound to pay the benefit in accordance with the terms of the deceased member's will, or if the member dies intestate in respect of the superannuation entitlement, then in accordance with the relevant intestacy rules.

Consequently, a will-maker may include a specific gift of their superannuation entitlements to one or more non-dependants, however the gift will only be effective if their entitlements first pass to their LPR, either as a result of a BDBN or the discretion of the SMSF trustee.

Form of payment

A PERSON'S DEATH BENEFIT may be paid out to a beneficiary as:

a one or more lump sums;
b one or more pensions; or
c a combination of the above.

However, only certain types of beneficiaries can receive particular types of benefits.

Under SIS regulation 6.21 (2A), a pension may only be paid to a dependant of the member, however if the dependant is a child of the member, the child must also be:

a under the age of 18;
b disabled under the Disability Services Act; or
c under the age of 25 and financially dependent on the deceased.

All other death benefit payments must take the form of a lump sum payment.

If a death benefit is paid in the form of a pension to the child of a deceased member where the child is under 25 and financially dependent on the deceased at the date of death of the member, it must be cashed as a lump sum no later than the time at which the child turns 25 (unless the child has a permanent disability).

The form of benefit that will be provided to a dependant can also create significant tax implications based on the type and mix of benefits chosen.

For example, it may be prudent to provide dependent children with a pension as they are taxed at adult rates. However, in the same context, it may not be appropriate to set aside a significant part of the death benefit to pay a pension to the child if that child must be paid the balance as a lump sum upon attaining the age of 25.

Taxation of death benefits

The manner in which a death benefit is taxed will differ depending on a number of factors, including whether:

- a the payment is a lump sum or a pension payment;
- b it is made to a death benefit dependant or a non-dependant; and
- c it comprises a tax free component or taxable component (or a proportion of both).

The definition of a 'death benefit dependant' is contained in the Tax Act and is different to the definition contained in the SIS Act.

A death benefit dependant of a person who has died is:

- a the deceased person's spouse or former spouse;
- b the deceased person's child aged less than 18;
- c any other person with whom the deceased person had an interdependency relationship just before he or she died; or
- d any other person who was a dependant of the deceased person just before he or she died.

'Interdependency relationship' has the same definition as in section 10A of the SIS Act.

The main difference between the SIS Act and Tax Act definitions of dependant is that the Tax Act does not consider a child over 18 to be a dependant unless they are disabled or they were under 25 and financially dependent on the deceased at the date of death.

Death benefits paid to adult children who do not otherwise qualify as tax dependants will be taxed on the payment as a non-dependant.

Importantly, it is only the taxable component of a benefit that is potentially subject to tax. The tax-free component (as the name would suggest) is always tax free in the recipient's hands, irrespective of whether the recipient is a dependant or non-dependant.

Lump Sum Payments

A lump sum death benefit payment made to a death benefit dependant will be tax free.

Where a dependant was originally receiving a pension and cashes out the balance of their entitlement as a result of turning 25, the lump sum payment will be tax free even though they do not fulfil the definition of a death benefit dependant under the Tax Act.

In relation to lump sum payments made to non-dependants, the taxation treatment depends upon whether the payment comprises a tax free component, a taxable component or a combination of both.

As noted above, the tax free component passes without taxation.

The tax free component includes contributions that have not been taxed (e.g. non-concessional contributions) and crystallised 30 June 2007 amounts (pre-July 83 component, undeducted contributions, post-30 June 1994 invalidity component, concessional component and CGT exempt component).

The balance of any payment will then be the taxable component. The taxable component then has two elements:

a the element taxed; and
b the element untaxed.

Although generally the taxable component will be comprised entirely of a taxed element, an untaxed element will arise if insurance is used to fund part of the death benefit.

The element taxed of a lump sum death benefit paid to a non-dependant is included in assessable income of the non-dependant, with a tax offset to ensure that the rate of tax on the element taxed does not exceed 15%.

The element untaxed of a lump sum death benefit paid to a non-dependant is included in assessable income with a tax offset to ensure that the rate of tax on the element untaxed in the fund does not exceed 30%.

As the Medicare levy applies to both the element taxed and element untaxed, the effective tax rates become 16.5% and 31.5% respectively.

Pension Payment

Income streams can only be paid to dependants.

As is the case with lump sum benefits, the tax free component of a death benefit pension is tax free.

The following table outlines the tax treatment for the two elements of the taxable component on the payment to a dependant of an income stream or pension.

Description	Tax treatment
The dependant is aged 60 or over	Element taxed is tax free. Element untaxed is included in the dependant's assessable income. Dependant receives a 10% tax offset.
The deceased member is aged 60 or over and the dependant is any age	Element untaxed is included in the dependant's assessable income. Dependant receives a 10% tax offset.
Both the deceased member and the dependant are under 60	Element taxed is included in the dependant's assessable income. Dependant receives a 15% tax offset. Element untaxed is included in the dependant's assessable income.

Other considerations

In addition to the tax related issues outlined above, a number of rules are potentially relevant in the context of death and superannuation.

The four main issues in this regard are:

a the proportioning rule;
b the inability to pay pensions to non-dependants;
c the taxation treatment of benefits paid to non-dependant children; and
d payments via the estate, and the use of testamentary trusts.

Proportioning rule

The proportioning rule requires that any superannuation benefit when paid is taken to comprise tax free and taxable components in the same proportions as they bear to the member's superannuation entitlements.

Without this rule, when paying a death benefit there would be an incentive to distribute:

a tax-free components to non-tax dependants; and
b taxable components to tax dependants.

The rule effectively results in the taxable portion of the death benefit that is paid to a non-tax dependant being subject to tax.

The only way in which this outcome can be avoided within a single fund is to ensure all payments are made to death benefit dependants.

An alternative approach is commonly referred to as the 're-contribution strategy' and involves:

a establishing a second fund for the member during their lifetime;
b ensuring that only contributions, transfers and roll-overs which would give rise to a tax-free component are made to the new

fund, while all other contributions are made to the existing fund; and

- over time, withdrawing funds from the first fund (either as lump sums or as a pension) and making after-tax contributions to the second fund.

As the second fund is comprised of almost entirely tax-free components (the earnings in the fund will create a taxable component), this fund can then be used to pay death benefits to non-tax dependants.

Obviously this approach will not work in all cases, and requires the establishment of a second fund with the associated administrative costs. The strategy can however provide some scope to at least reduce the tax that non-dependants might otherwise incur if a single fund approach was adopted.

It should be noted that separate and distinct funds are required for this approach, as the ATO does not accept that separate accounts within the same superannuation fund have the benefit of separate treatment under the proportioning rule.

The application of the general anti-avoidance rules under part IVA of the Tax Act also need to be considered.

No pensions to non-dependants

The requirement to pay lump sums to non-tax dependants coupled with the proportioning rule ensures that tax will always be payable on the taxable component of a death benefit paid to a non-tax dependant.

In this context, a child who does not qualify for receipt of a pension as set out above cannot be paid a pension, even if the child otherwise qualifies as a tax dependant.

Therefore, even where a member is fully supporting an adult child, unless that child is considered disabled under the Disability Services Act (or is under 25 and financially dependent on the deceased member at the date of death), the child must take any benefit as a lump sum.

Although as a financial dependant a child will not be taxed on the lump sum benefit paid to them, the inability to take the benefit as a pension limits the availability of concessional tax treatment on the income stream. This is because any income stream derived by that child on investment of the lump sum benefit will be taxed in their hands at their marginal tax rate.

Non-dependant children

One of the well known anomalies with the payment of a death benefit is the difference in the tax treatment where a member aged 60 or over is able to 'predict' the timing of their death.

When a member is over 60 years of age, generally all super benefits will be tax-free on withdrawal prior to death.

In contrast, the same benefits distributed as a death payment can be liable for tax of up to 30% (plus Medicare and other surcharges).

Therefore, if the member of an SMSF knows exactly (or even approximately) when they will die, they would withdraw their entire benefit as a lump sum before death, pay no tax, and either pay the benefit to their child, or leave it to fall into their estate to be paid to the child under the will, or to their ultimate benefit via a testamentary trust.

On the other hand, where a member dies unexpectedly, the death benefit paid to that same child is subject to tax in the hands of the child as set out above.

This results in a de facto death duty being imposed on individuals who die unexpectedly, with adult children receiving their superannuation entitlements.

Obviously, there are a range of competing issues that need to be considered as part of any superannuation and estate planning exercise, however there seems to be an increasing trend for SMSF members to actively review the total amount they wish to retain in an SMSF in their later years.

For those wishing to limit the amount of tax payable on death, there is a bias to withdrawing amounts from superannuation fund prior to death.

This said, if a member withdraws too much, the contribution caps will limit how much (if any) they can re-contribute to superannuation and the income earned on investment outside super will not enjoy concessional tax treatment.

In particular, where a member withdraws their entire benefit as a lump sum, any earnings and subsequent capital gains on these investments will occur outside the super environment and will not be concessionally taxed – that is, they will be taxed at the marginal rates of tax. Where benefits are retained in the superannuation environment, with pensions continuing, any earnings, capital gains and pension payments will be tax-free.

While some advisers argue that it is possible to 'pre-sign' a super benefits withdrawal form to enable it to be dated by someone after the member's death (the date would be some time before death).

Practically however, and ignoring the question of fraud, the ATO requires physical withdrawal in order to avoid the imposition of tax and therefore 'pre-signing' withdrawal forms is an ineffective strategy.

Payments to the estate and testamentary trusts

Where a death benefit is paid to an estate (via the LPR), a 'look-through' approach is adopted and the tax treatment is largely the same as for direct payments.

In other words, the tax treatment depends upon who ultimately receives the benefit from the estate – to the extent that tax dependants receive the benefit, it will be tax free.

Where non-tax dependants receive the benefit, it will be taxed according to the various components as set out above and the trustee of the estate will be liable to account for tax on the benefit.

If the entitlements pass to a testamentary trust, there is a risk the proceeds will be treated as passing to a non-dependant unless appropriate safeguards are in place.

Specifically, assuming the testamentary trust has a broad range of eligible beneficiaries (which may include both death benefit dependants and non-dependants), then the will should ideally include discretion for the trustee to segregate or quarantine the superannuation entitlements for the benefit of the death benefit dependants only.

Alternatively, the will could create multiple testamentary trusts with one testamentary trust being established specifically to receive the superannuation entitlements, again with the range of beneficiaries being limited to death benefit dependants of the will-maker.

As a third alternative, in some circumstances it might also be appropriate to have the death benefit paid directly death benefit dependants rather than the estate.

CGT and death benefit in specie distributions

SPECIAL CONSIDERATION MUST be given to the succession issues around an SMSF where non-liquid assets such as real estate are owned.

The ownership of property via an SMSF can have many advantages, including:

a. the members effectively pay rent to themselves, which is deductible to the payer. The SMSF enjoys concessional tax treatment, so the net income is taxed at a maximum rate of 15%;
b. a limited recourse borrowing arrangement (as explained earlier) can be used to effectively allow the SMSF to borrow to fund the acquisition;
c. any gain ultimately on the sale of the property will be taxed at a maximum rate of 10% (assuming the property has been held for 12 months); and
d. once the member enters pension phase and the property is used to support the pension payment, no tax is payable on the net income or capital gain.

However issues commonly arise where an SMSF owns the business real property from which the members (or an entity they control) operate their business.

In particular, problems can arise if the member wishes to retain the property with a view to passing it to the next generation, such as where the business itself is intended to pass to the next generation.

The SIS Act requires a death benefit to be paid to a beneficiary. If the benefit can be paid, say, as a pension to the surviving spouse, this may delay the need in the short term to deal with the underlying asset. However, at some future point (on the death of the spouse), there will be a need to deal with the asset.

If member dies in pension phase and their pension pass to a dependant beneficiary, then the dependant may either:

a continue receiving pension payments tax free; or
b exercise their entitlement to a lump sum payment equal to the value of the underlying pension asset.

The alternative approach of transferring the asset to a beneficiary can cause a number of revenue related issues, including:

a there are no proceeds from the disposal of the asset, so the SMSF must find other resources to meet the tax liability;
b stamp duty will generally be payable. In a sale, stamp duty is usual paid by the purchaser. With an in specie transfer, the parties will need to decide who pays the stamp duty liability. Again this will have to be funded separately as there are no proceeds from disposal;
c depending on the circumstances of the beneficiary, there may be tax to pay on receipt of the property as a superannuation death benefit. Again, because no cash proceeds are received, this tax needs to be funded independently.

Having the beneficiary as a member (or making them a member after the deceased member's death) does potentially solve the problems outlined above. This approach will however only assist if there are sufficient other assets to pay the death benefit. If this is the case then the property could support the continuing member's benefit, with other assets being paid out.

The key requirement is that the death benefit be paid – members cannot simply leave the benefit in the SMSF indefinitely.

SPTs

A SPT is a trust that is established solely to receive the superannuation benefits of a member following death. A SPT can be established by a will or by deed after the death of an individual.

Generally, the beneficiaries of a SPT must be confined to persons who are 'death benefit dependants' of the deceased, as explained above.

The benefits of having a SPT in a will are:

a. it provides greater asset protection compared to the superannuation death benefits being paid directly to a death benefit dependant - for example, against relationship breakdowns, creditors or spendthrift beneficiaries;
b. distributions from the SPT will generally be 'excepted trust income' – this means that recipients under the age of 18 will be treated as adults for tax purposes;
c. the distribution of the superannuation death benefits to the SPT is taxed in the same way as if they had been paid directly to the death benefit dependant (provided the beneficiaries of the SPT are limited to tax dependants).

Generally, most advisers draft the terms of testamentary trusts such that the range of potential beneficiaries listed are significantly wider than dependants for tax purposes. Specialist advisers will however also generally craft the testamentary trust so that the trustee has complete discretion about which of the beneficiaries may receive any superannuation benefits available for distribution.

In particular, the terms of the will allow the trustee to essentially establish a 'sub trust' of the testamentary trust for receipt of the superannuation proceeds – with the only beneficiaries being those who satisfy the definition of a tax dependant.

In this way, the various benefits of having a SPT, as outlined above, can be achieved.

If the trustee chooses to utilise a SPT, an example of how the estate assets could flow is as follows:

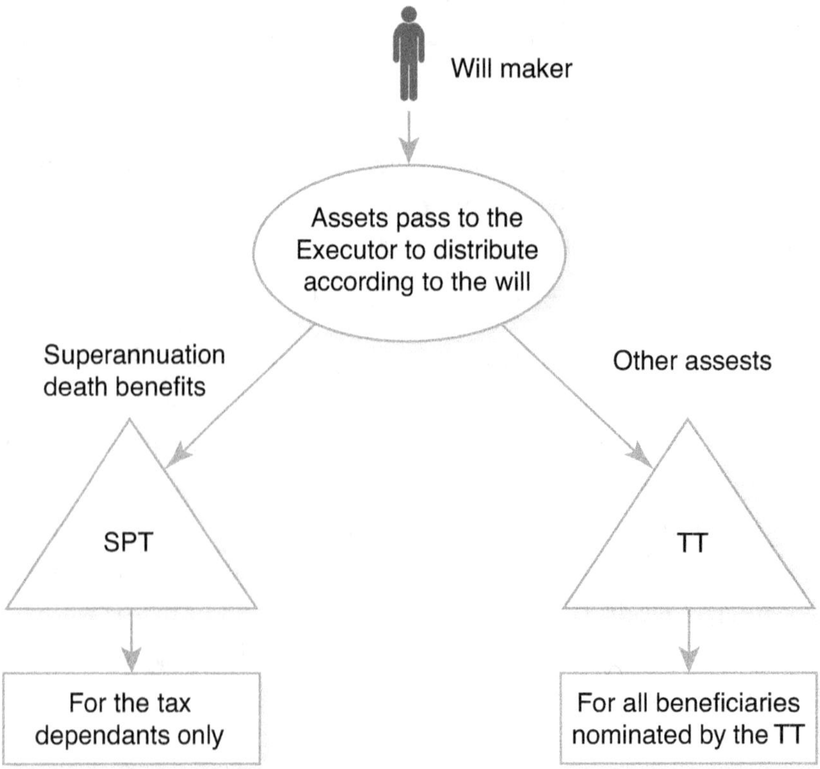

SPTs established outside a will

SPTs MAY ALSO be established outside a will, after the death of a will maker, where the deceased's will does not contain a testamentary trust with the features mentioned above. This style of SPT is of particular benefit to a surviving spouse with infant children, where tax effective income splitting is important.

For example:

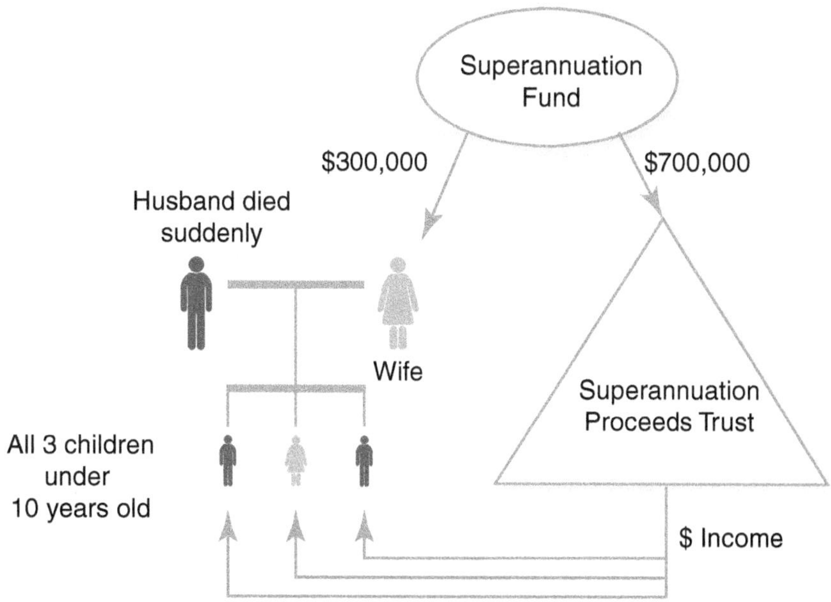

Following the death of the husband, the wife in default of any other decision by the trustee of the SMSF would be entitled to receive his $1 million superannuation death benefit.

The wife, in her capacity as trustee of the SMSF distributes $700,000 to a SPT she establishes and controls.

Income and capital distributions to the infant children can then be used to pay for food, accommodation, school fees, clothing, holidays etc.

Each year the wife is able to distribute approximately $22,000 to each of the three children (i.e. over $65,000) tax free, under the excepted trust income rules of the Tax Act.

There are a number of technical provisions that need to be satisfied to ensure access to this outcome.

Generally, an SPT established following the death of a member of an SMSF is significantly more restrictive than an SPT established pursuant to the terms of the former member's will, for example:

a minor beneficiaries (persons under 18 years of age on establishment of the SPT) must be the ultimate capital beneficiaries of the SPT, meaning the assets of the trust must ultimately vest in them;
b the transfer of benefits must generally occur within 3 calendar years of the date of death of the deceased;
c the concessional rates of tax will generally not be available to the grandchildren of a member; and
d depending on the situation, the assets transferred must not exceed the entitlements that the minor beneficiaries would have received if the deceased SMSF member had not left a valid will (i.e. if the deceased had died intestate).

Use of nominations

As outlined above, death benefits do not automatically form part of a person's estate.

Rather, the trustee of the member's superannuation fund is responsible for the distribution of death benefits.

A member can regulate the manner in which their entitlements are paid in two ways:

a through the use of death benefit nominations; or

b by regulating control of the SMSF, thereby determining who will have the discretion to pay the death benefits following the member's death.

c In virtually every estate planning exercise, the issue of how members of an SMSF can direct payment of benefits, on death, invariably arises.

d Essentially a member of an SMSF has three main choices for specifying what should happen in relation to their superannuation entitlements on death (assuming the proposed recipient is entitled at law), namely:

  (i) nomination – the trustee is bound to deal with a member's benefit in their best interests. Before making a decision, the trustee will normally make enquiries as to the member's family situation, who their dependants are, the provisions of their will and other relevant circumstances;

  (ii) a non-BDBN – the trustee is not bound by a non-binding notice and has an absolute discretion as to where the death benefit will be paid. Where a non-binding notice is made, it should be taken into account as part of any decision by the trustee as to how to distribute the benefit; and

  (iii) a BDBN – the trustee is obliged to distribute a member's death benefits in accordance with a valid BDBN.

BDBNs have the potential to allow members to protect their death benefits from disputes; where there is no nomination or a non-binding one, a trustee's decision can be challenged.

BDBNs can also be used as part of a member's overall estate plan - for example, as part of a tax planning strategy for infant children or as an asset protection strategy for adult children.

A BDBN is essentially an election made by a member that is binding on the trustee, whereby the trustee agrees to direct any benefits remaining in a member's superannuation account in the way that the member has instructed.

If the trust fund of the SMSF allows it, a member may make a BDBN. The trustee is legally bound to comply with a valid BDBN. That is the trustee has no discretion to pay death benefits other than in accordance with the notice.

A BDBN must be made strictly in compliance with the requirements of the relevant trust deed to be effective and if the trust deed does not permit BDBNs, any purported BDBN by the member is unlikely to be upheld by a Court if challenged.

Below is an example of some of the requirements that are generally set out in a trust deed as needing to be satisfied before a nomination will be held to be binding (the first three of which are expressly required by legislation):

'Any binding death benefit nomination:

a *must be in writing;*
b *must be signed and dated by the member in the presence of two adult witnesses;*
c *must contain a declaration signed and dated by the witnesses that the member signed the notice in their presence;*
d *will not lapse with the passing of time;*
e *may be revoked by the member by written notice to the trustee at any time;*
f *must contain sufficient details to identify the member; and*
g *must contain sufficient details to identify the beneficiaries.'*

While almost all trust deeds that allow BDBNs will have provisions along the lines outlined above, at times there will be additional provisions that are not necessarily expected. Some examples in this regard can include:

a a prohibition on amending the trust deed for the SMSF in a way that impacts on the BDBN;
b a provision that empowers the trustee to accept amended BDBNs from the financial attorney of a member;
c the trustee may be required to consider and accept a BDBN before it is valid; and
d there may be a particular table or form that is required to be embedded into the BDBN, which sets out the percentage entitlement of each beneficiary.

Although BDBNs can provide greater certainty to members of where their superannuation is to be distributed once they die, they also create a lack of flexibility, particularly for any change in circumstances.

For instance, a BDBN may result in unfavourable tax outcomes for the beneficiaries if it is not reviewed and updated following changes to the tax laws affecting death benefits.

In addition, a BDBN is only binding on the trustee if the death benefits are directed to the member's LPR or dependants.

Historically, BDBNs expired after 3 years if they were not confirmed and in many funds, this is still the case. More recent deeds however allow non-lapsing BDBNs to be made, which will continue indefinitely unless expressly revoked by the member.

If a BDBN expires without being renewed, the trustee is free to distribute the relevant money any way they like (so long as it is permitted under the fund's deed and superannuation law).

As is the case with wills, BDBNs should also be updated or confirmed when there is a significant change in a person's circumstances, such as divorce, death and additional children.

A non-binding death benefit nomination, as its name suggests, does not obligate a trustee to make a payment and are merely a guide. The trustee retains a discretion (subject to the terms of the deed) as to how the death benefit is paid.

The main disadvantage of a BDBN is the inability of a trustee to rectify the situation where the member has not kept the nomination up to date, particularly where there has been a significant change in the circumstances of the member.

If a member is unlikely to keep their nomination up to date, a non-BDBN allows the trustee to consider these factors in deciding how the death benefit should be paid and is often more appropriate.

When should BDBN be used?

BROADLY, A BDBN will be useful in the following circumstances:

a people in second or third marriages;
b where there are children from different relationships;
c where there are concerns about beneficiaries challenging the estate.

The main advantage of making a BDBN is the certainty it provides.

By completing a BDBN the risk of challenges to the fund that might arise on the member's death are minimised.

The main disadvantage of making a BDBN is that the nomination locks the trustee of the SMSF into directing any death benefits to the dependants or to the LPR nominated. If a person's circumstances change, for instance, due to divorce, separation or bankruptcy, the certainty that was hoped for might be negated.

A few critical points to remember in this area include the following:

a If a member's circumstances change and they have failed to update their BDBN, it will, subject in some situations to automatic lapsing (for example, every three years), continue to be binding on the trustee.
b As noted above, trust deed for the SMSF must allow for a BDBN to be given to the trustee of the fund – even some recently set up deeds do not always have such a provision.
c Unless specifically provided for in the SMSF trust deed, a BDBN will often need to be 'refreshed' every three years. An alternate approach is to update the trust deed for the SMSF to 'hardwire' the nomination into the deed, avoiding the requirement to regularly refresh the nomination (often referred to as a 'superannuation will', as explained in more detail).

d Where this is done, the fact that there might be other nominations, or even provisions in a person's will, not be of any effect–rather the terms of the SMSF trust deed must be followed.

Superannuation wills

ANOTHER APPROACH, SIMILAR to BDBNs is the use of 'superannuation wills'.

This terminology can be somewhat misleading as the document is not a 'will' in the ordinary meaning, and different organisations can be referring to different approaches when they refer to 'superannuation wills'.

In general however, a 'superannuation will' involves amending the trust deed for the SMSF to embed the nomination of beneficiaries within that document, rather than relying on a stand-alone nomination.

For instance, the trust deed may be amended to specify that a particular member's death benefits must be paid to their LPR upon the death.

The deed will then commonly also contain provisions preventing any amendments from being made to the death benefit provisions of the deed, after a member's death.

This approach is only available for SMSFs and can be very inflexible (if a member later wishes to vary their nomination, the entire deed must be amended), however in the appropriate circumstances it can be a powerful tool for ensuring the member's wishes are followed.

The 'read the deed' mantra, which is so often used in the context of family trusts, is of similar importance in relation to superannuation wills. One particular provision to be aware of in this regard is that, even if a nomination (which appears to be binding) is embedded under the SMSF trust deed, unless the provision of that deed has a prohibition against amendment, the intentions of the parties may not in fact be achieved.

For example, the remaining trustees after death could elect to vary the SMSF trust deed (and effectively remove the BDBN) before ultimately making a death benefit payment as they determine.

There are a number of limitations surrounding what actions an attorney can take on behalf of a donor under an enduring power of attorney.

One transaction that is not dealt with expressly in the superannuation or attorney legislation is whether a BDBN can be made, changed, revoked or refreshed.

The conservative position is that any step in relation to a BDBN is a personal power, and therefore cannot be delegated to an attorney.

This said, the preferred view seems to be that so long as the attorney is given power under the enduring power of attorney, and the trust deed for the superannuation fund does not otherwise contain any prohibitions, then an attorney may take steps in relation to a BDBN, so long as they believe that it is in the best interests of the donor.

This line of reasoning is supported by SCT determination No. D-7-084/030.

It also appears to be relatively widely accepted that an attorney may be able to 'affirm' an existing BDBN that has lapsed, again so long as there is an express power in the attorney appointment document.

Reversionary pensions

WHERE A MEMBER has reached preservation age, and is already receiving their superannuation benefit as an income stream, it is possible to nominate a reversionary beneficiary that requires upon the member's death, that the income stream continues to be paid as they have directed.

Historically, the ATO sought to argue that a pension (and the tax exemption thereon) ceased as soon as the member in receipt of the pension died.

The exception to this position was where a dependent beneficiary of the deceased was automatically entitled under the super fund's deed, or rules of the pension, to receive the pension on the death of the member. This type of pension is often referred to as an ARP.

The Federal Government, however, announced that, with effect from 1 July 2012, a tax exemption applies following the death of an SMSF member in receipt of a pension until that pension has been paid out of the fund. The main requirement for the exemption to apply is that the pension is paid out of the fund as soon as practicable.

As a result, an ARP is not required to ensure access to the tax exemption.

Some confusion can also arise where a member has put in place both an ARP and a BDBN, with conflicting outcomes.

In these circumstances, the provisions of the trust deed are critical for determining whether the ARP or the BDBN should prevail, and it will often be the case that the ARP will take precedence over an inconsistent BDBN.

Where there is a BDBN in place for superannuation savings that are also the subject of a reversionary pension, it will be necessary to determine which takes priority.

Best practice dictates that both documents articulate which has priority, or at least that whichever document is signed most recently applies.

Where however there is limited guidance addressing the issue, it is generally accepted that the reversionary pension will take precedence over the BDBN. The reasons for this include:

a. A valid reversionary pension would automatically remove the deceased member's death benefits from a fund, and therefore, any BDBN will have no assets to attach to.
b. The ATO has confirmed via its national tax liaison group committee that the preferred interpretation (subject to any specific provisions to the contrary) is that the pension does take priority.

Practically, in most client specific situations, the approach adopted has always been that the reversionary pension takes priority.

Case law

THE ISSUES WHICH commonly arise when structuring an estate plan for superannuation benefits are highlighted in the following court decisions, summarised below.

Katz v Grossman [2005] NSWSC 934

Although from 2005, one of the most famous cases in this area remains *Katz v Grossman*.

The case highlights how important it is to ensure an appropriate trustee is appointed for an SMSF and how control of the SMSF should be one of the specific issues identified for consideration when reviewing an estate plan.

The case involved Katz bringing an action against his sister Grossman (and her husband), claiming an interest in their father's SMSF.

The facts were as follows:

a the mother and father were the original individual trustees and members of the SMSF;

b the mother died some years before the father, and subsequently Grossman (the daughter) was appointed as a co-trustee with her father to ensure that the SMSF continued to comply with the relevant superannuation legislation;

c when the father subsequently died, Grossman appointed her husband as a co-trustee with her;

d prior to his death, the father had made a non-BDBN indicating that he wanted his superannuation entitlements divided equally between Katz (his son) and Grossman;

e the father's will also divided all his assets equally between Katz and Grossman; and

f Grossman (and her husband) ignored the nomination and will and paid the entire superannuation entitlements, totalling approximately $1 million, to herself.

The Court held that:

a all the trustees of the SMSF had been validly appointed at the relevant times;
b as the nomination signed by the father was a non-BDBN, the trustee was entitled to elect not to follow it; and
c the trustee therefore had full discretion to determine how the entitlements should be paid, including the discretion to pay the full amount to Grossman to the exclusion of Katz.

As a result, the challenge by Katz was unsuccessful and Grossman was entitled to keep the superannuation entitlements, notwithstanding the father's apparent intention that Katz and Grossman share equally in all his assets, including the superannuation benefits.

Moss Super Pty Ltd v Hayne [2008] VSC 158

This case involved a dispute around an attempted change of trustee of an SMSF following the death of a member.

In particular, the surviving member purported to change the trusteeship of the SMSF, so that a company of which she was the sole shareholder and director would be appointed.

The trust deed set out the process by which a change of trusteeship could take place and specifically required the 'founder' to appoint any new trustee.

While the sole director of the new trustee company was also the founder, she did not in fact sign the change of trustee documentation in her capacity as founder.

In other words, while she signed in her capacity as the sole director of the new trustee, there was no provision where she also signed in her founder role.

Critically, the Court found that where structures are created in which individuals have multiple roles to play, the requirements around those roles must be respected and complied with. This meant the attempted change of trusteeship was invalid.

Notaras v Notaras [2012] NSWSC 947

In this case, two brothers were the trustees and members of an SMSF.

Over time, one of the brothers (Brinos) made withdrawals from the SMSF, of which around $60,000 were alleged to be in excess of his entitlement.

Brinos' brother (Basil) had no knowledge of the withdrawals and thus had not provided consent.

Basil approached the Court to seek an order that Brinos be removed as the trustee of the SMSF due to his failure to act jointly, and that he be replaced with a corporate trustee (Bazport Pty Ltd), of which Basil was the sole director and secretary.

The Court accepted Basil's argument appointed Bazport Pty Ltd as the co-trustee in place of Brinos, leaving the SMSF with both an individual and corporate trustee.

The Court confirmed Basil would (as a result of the decision) need approval from the Tax Office for its failure to comply with the superannuation law requirement for all members of an SMSF to also be trustees.

Ioppolo & Hesford v Conti & Anor [2013] WASC 389

Ioppolo v Conti provides another example of how unintended consequences can arise where the control of an SMSF is not properly considered as part of a member's estate plan.

The situation was as follows:

a the husband and wife originally established an SMSF and were the individual trustees;
b the wife died and left a will directing her LPR to pay her superannuation benefits to her children. The will specifically excluded her husband from receiving those benefits;
c the wife had not signed any form of binding or non-binding

death benefit nomination prior to her death;

d following the wife's death, the husband retired as trustee and appointed a corporate trustee in his place. He was the sole director and shareholder of the corporate trustee; and

e the corporate trustee then resolved to pay the entirety of the wife's superannuation entitlements (of approximately $650,000) to the husband, as opposed to her LPR pursuant to her will.

The executors of the will challenged the distribution and argued that the husband failed to act in a 'bona fide manner' in light of the provision in the will. They claimed that the husband should have appointed the executors as replacement trustees for the SMSF, rather than the corporate trustee with himself as the sole director.

The Court dismissed the executor's claim and allowed the husband to retain all of the wife's superannuation entitlements.

The Court confirmed that there is no obligation under the superannuation legislation for a surviving trustee to automatically appoint the executors of a former co-trustee as replacement trustees of an SMSF.

In addition, of particular relevance to advisers, the Court specifically noted that:

a the husband had sought specialist advice in relation to his rights and obligations as the trustee;

b the husband had deliberately waived his right to confidentiality (or privilege) in relation to this advice;

c the Court on reviewing the advice agreed with the conclusion given, being that the husband was able to make the payment to himself;

d where a trustee is acting on the advice of a specialist, it will generally be very difficult to successfully argue that the trustee lacked good faith in making the decision; and

e ultimately, a Court will only review the way in which the discretion of a trustee is exercised in very limited circumstances.

Wooster v Morris [2013] VSC 594

*Wooster v Morris explores some of the key issues around the enforceability of a binding death benefit nomination (**BDBN**).*

The facts of the case were as follows:

- a a husband and wife were the trustees and members of an SMSF;
- b the husband had two adult daughters from a previous relationship;
- c the husband had made a BDBN in favour of his adult daughters, who were also the executors of his will;
- d the husband's wife, following his death, sought to challenge the BDBN on the basis that the trust deed required it to be delivered to her and she claimed that it had not been;
- e as the wife was the sole surviving trustee and was able to regulate the appointment of the new trustee (ignoring the claims of the daughters as executors of the will), she paid the entire death benefit (being approximately $925,000) to herself.

The husband's daughters challenged the distribution and the Court ultimately ordered the wife to return all funds.

The Court also ordered the wife to contribute personally to the costs of the litigation (which were in the vicinity of $350,000), as these costs would otherwise have significantly depleted the balance of the superannuation entitlements being received by the adult daughters.

McIntosh v McIntosh [2014] QSC 99

The facts of this case were:

- a a father and mother had a son, James, prior to their separation. By all reports, the relationship between the father and mother was acrimonious following the separation;
- b James died without a will, meaning his parents were entitled to his estate in equal shares under the intestacy rules;
- c his mother applied for and was granted letters of administration;
- d James had around $450,000 in a superannuation fund and did not have a valid binding death benefit nomination at the date

of his death, although he had a non-BDBN in favour of his mother;

e his mother applied to the trustee of the superannuation fund to have the entitlements paid to herself absolutely, rather than to herself in her capacity as administrator of the estate. This meant his mother would receive 100% of the entitlements, rather than the 50% she would have received from the estate; and

f his father challenged the mother's actions and argued that she was breaching her obligations as administrator to maximise the value of the estate.

The Court found in the father's favour and held that the mother had clear fiduciary duties as administrator to act in the best interests of the estate, and she had failed these duties by preferring her own interests over those of the estate.

The Court ordered the mother to pay the superannuation entitlements to the estate.

While there are obviously a number of issues in relation to this case, three critical steps that could have been taken are as follows:

a To the extent that they were available, BDBNS could have been made to the mother personally (in this regard, non-BDBNs had in fact been made nominating the mother solely).

b With the aid of hindsight, the mother should not have applied to administer the deceased estate. This would have relieved her of any duty to act in the best interests of the estate and therefore she could have proceeded to make the application for superannuation benefits to be paid to her personally without her actions being challenged.

c The son should have made a will at least appointing his mother as executor (this would have potentially meant that she did not have any conflict of interest as the son would have been deemed to have been aware of the potential when making the nomination). Ideally, the will would have also nominated the mother as the sole beneficiary of the estate – thereby meaning that even if the funds were not paid to her directly, she should have ultimately received them in any event.

Whether the superannuation death benefits can be regulated via a will was considered by the SCT in D11-12/066 where the deceased failed to execute a BDBN or a non-BDBN.

Instead she executed a will which appointed her spouse, son and daughter as LPR and left a specific bequest to her spouse.

The trustee of the fund was of the opinion that in the absence of a BDBN, the entire superannuation benefit had to be paid to the LPR of the deceased, to be distributed in accordance with the terms of the will.

The deceased's spouse challenged this decision arguing that it was unfair and unreasonable given the deceased had left a specific bequest in her will to her. The spouse argued that this bequest constituted a death benefit direction.

The SCT found that the decision of the trustee to distribute the superannuation benefit to the deceased's LPR was not unfair, unreasonable or contrary to law. The trustee's decision was in accordance with the terms of the deed and the superannuation law and this, according to the SCT, was the correct decision.

The decision highlights the importance of standalone nominations and that it is unlikely a provision in a will can ever constitute a valid nomination.

Appendix One

MODEL SMSF TRUST DEED

Overview

On signing this deed the Trustee establishes a superannuation fund (**Fund**) to:

a provide superannuation benefits for the Members and their Dependants on the death of a Member; and
b allow for any other purposes permitted by the Law.

The Trustee confirms it will:

a act as trustee of the Fund;
b exercise its powers in accordance with this document; and
c ensure the Fund enjoys any income tax concessions available to superannuation funds.

Agreed terms

1 Fund

1.1 This document confirms:

- **a** how the Fund must operate;
- **b** the responsibilities of the Trustee; and
- **c** the rights and responsibilities of those associated with the Fund.

2 Key details

2.1 The key details of the Fund are as follows.

Trustee	
Name of Fund	
Members	

Review notes

1. This fund is a self managed superannuation fund (SMSF).
2. The rules for the SMSF are set out in this document, normally referred to as a 'trust deed'.
3. Once the deed is signed, there are a number of steps that the Trustee is obliged to take and specialist advisers should be able to guide you through the various government requirements – there is an explanation of the main obligations in the Product Disclosure Statement (**PDS**).
4. The PDS should be read in conjunction with the trust deed.
5. If this deed is being adopted as part of an update to an existing trust deed, most statutory requirements will have already been met.
6. Throughout the trust deed, there are 'review notes' (in the same format as this wording) designed to provide further insight to the legal provisions.

7. The review notes do not form part of the legal provisions of the trust deed or any of the other ancillary documents such as the PDS.
8. If there is any confusion or conflict between the review notes and the provisions of the trust deed and schedules, the trust deed and schedules apply.
9. Importantly, the trust deed and schedules are subject to any other provisions in the Law. If there is ever any doubt as to the appropriate approach to take, specialist advice should be obtained.
10. The PDS is a document that is designed to provide guidance in relation to all of the fundamental aspects of an SMSF.
11. It is also not legally binding as such (although it is compulsory to provide a PDS to each Member of an SMSF).
12. As the PDS is itself designed to be an information document, it does not have any review notes.

3 Definitions

3.1 In this document:

Term	Definition
Account	Means any account established by the Trustee under this document, including the following: (a) Accumulation Account; (b) Pension Account; (c) Income Account; (d) Floating Account; (e) Forfeiture Account; (f) Reserve Account; and (g) any other accounts required to be opened or maintained by the Trustee under the Law.

Term	Definition
Accumulation Account	Means the account established by the Trustee.
Allocated Pension	Has the same meaning as in the SIS Regulations.
Allot	Has the same meaning as in the SIS Regulations.
Annuity	Has the same meaning as in the Law.
Anti-detriment Payment	Means a Superannuation Lump Sum arising from the death of the Member to compensate the Fund for the Tax payable on Contributions.
Applicant	Means a Member who makes a contributions splitting application.
Approved Benefit Arrangement	Means a fund or benefit arrangement other than the Fund (including another Complying Superannuation Fund, an Approved Deposit Fund or an Annuity arrangement) into which or from which assets can be transferred from or into without causing the Fund to be in breach of the Law, including an Eligible Rollover Fund.
Approved Deposit Fund	Means a fund which is complying approved deposit fund under the Tax Act.
Auditor	Means the auditor of the Fund.
Beneficiary	Means a person who is presently and absolutely entitled to receive a Benefit including a Member, a Dependant or a Pensioner.
Benefit	Means any amount which is payable out of the Fund to or in respect of a Member.
Benefit Entitlement	Means any amount held in the Fund which may become payable to a person but to which the person has not become absolutely and indefeasibly entitled.

Term	Definition
BDBN	Means a nomination made by a Member for the payment or application of a death benefit that is binding on the Trustee under the Law.
Business Day	Means a day on which banks are open for general banking in the capital city of the State of the situs of the Fund.
Child	Has the same meaning as in the SIS Act and SIS Regulations.
Closing Date	Means the date the Fund is determined to be wound up, which must be on or before the date required by the Law.
Compassionate Grounds	Has the same meaning as in the SIS Act and SIS Regulations.
Complying Superannuation Fund	Means a fund which satisfies the definition of a complying superannuation fund under the Law.
Constitutional Corporation	Has the same meaning as in the Law.
Contribution	Means gross payments to the Fund in respect of Members, before the deduction of any Tax payable in respect of those payments and includes the transfer of an asset that is intended by the transferor to be a contribution.
Corporations Act	Means the *Corporations Act* 2001 *(Cth)*.
Dependant	Includes anyone who is a dependant as defined under the Law.
Directors	Means (where the Trustee is a Constitutional Corporation) the directors or board of management for the time being of the Trustee.

Term	Definition
Disclosure Document	Means any document required to be given under the Law to a person applying to be a Member.
Earnings	Means all net income and net capital gains derived from the assets of the Fund, whether realised or unrealised, after deducting any capital losses, allowances for expenses and Tax as the Trustee determines.
Eligible Rollover Fund	Has the same meaning as in the Law.
Employee	Has the same meaning as in the SIS Act and SIS Regulations.
Employer	Has the same meaning as in the SIS Act and SIS Regulations.
Financial Year	Means a period of 12 months ending on 30 June or any other period of 12 months as the Trustee determines.
Floating Account	Means the account established by the Trustee.
Forfeiture Account	Means the account established by the Trustee.
Fund	Means SMSF fund name.
Fund Earning Rate	Means the earning rate for the Fund (which may for the purposes of this document be negative) calculated by the Trustee after taking into account any provisions or reserves for future contingencies as the Trustee determines.
Gainful Employment	Means engagement in any business, trade, profession, vocation, calling, occupation or employment for gain to the extent required by the Law.

Term	Definition
Guarantee Act	Means the *Superannuation Guarantee Charge Act 1992* (Cth), the *Superannuation Guarantee (Administration) Act 1992* (Cth) and any regulations made to those Acts.
Income Account	Means the account established by the Trustee.
Income Stream	Means: (a) a Pension; (b) an Annuity; or (c) a Benefit payable in a form other than as a Superannuation Lump Sum, as allowed under the Law.
Individual Trustee	Means a natural person who is appointed to be a Trustee of the Fund.
Insurer	Means any insurer with whom the Trustee effects any Policy.
Law	Means any requirement under the following acts and regulations: (a) SIS Act; (b) SIS Regulations; (c) *Family Law Act 1975* (Cth); (d) *Family Law (Superannuation) Regulations 2001* (Cth); (e) Corporations Act; (f) *Corporations Regulations 2001* (Cth); (g) Tax Act; and (h) any other legislation which the Trustee must comply with for the Fund to: (i) qualify for concessional Tax treatment as a Complying Superannuation Fund; or (ii) meet any other requirement of a Statutory Authority.
LPR	Has the same meaning as in the SIS Act.

Term	Definition
Levy	Includes a levy payable by the Fund in accordance with the *Superannuation Supervisory Levy Act 1991* (Cth), the *Superannuation (Fund Assistance Levy) Act 1993* (Cth) and any other legislation or regulations which impose levies on the Fund.
Maximum Splittable Amount	Has the same meaning as in the SIS Regulations.
Member	Means a person who has been admitted as a member of the Fund and has not ceased to be a member of the Fund.
Member Account	Means an Accumulation Account or Pension Account as the context requires.
Nominated Beneficiary	Means any Dependant or LPR of a Member, nominated by the Member.
Non-BDBN	Means a nomination made by a Member in relation to the payment or application of a death benefit that is not a BDBN.
Non-Member Spouse	Has the same meaning as in the SIS Act and SIS Regulations. A person ceases to be a Non-Member Spouse when: (a) the entitlement of the Non-Member Spouse in respect of a Payment Split is paid out of the Fund; or (b) they become a Member.
Payment Flag	Has the same meaning as in the Law.
Payment Split	Has the same meaning as in the Law.
Pension	Includes a Benefit paid in accordance with the meaning of 'pension' under the Law.
Pension Account	Means the account established by the Trustee.

Term	Definition
Pensioner	Means a Member who is entitled to receive or has applied to receive Benefits payable to the Member as a Pension, including a Reversionary Beneficiary in receipt of a Pension.
Permanent Incapacity	Has the same meaning as in the Law.
Permitted Entity	Means any person or entity permitted under the Law to make a contribution in respect of a Member.
Policy	Means any policy of assurance including a policy on the life of a Member for endowment, term, disablement, accident or sickness insurance.
Preservation Age	Has the same meaning as in the SIS Regulations.
Preserved	Means being subject to the prohibition against paying any amount from the Fund before a Member: (a) reaches Preservation Age; or (b) is otherwise entitled to be paid that amount under the Law.
Reserve Account	Means the account established by the Trustee.
Retires from Employment	Means enters into retirement as defined under the Law for the payment of Benefits.
Retires from Gainful Employment	Means enters actual retirement from Gainful Employment or Retires from Employment.
Reversionary Beneficiary	Means a Dependant nominated by a Pensioner (and in default of a nomination by the Pensioner, where appropriate, a Dependant nominated by the Trustee) who is eligible to receive a Benefit on the death of a Pensioner.

Term	Definition
Self managed Superannuation Fund	Means a superannuation fund which satisfies the requirements of a self managed superannuation fund set out under the Law.
Severe Financial Hardship	Has the same meaning as in the SIS Act and SIS Regulations.
Shortfall Component	Has the same meaning as in the Guarantee Act.
SIS Act	Means the *Superannuation Industry (Supervision) Act 1993* (Cth).
SIS Regulations	Means any regulations made under the SIS Act.
Split	Means to rollover or transfer out of the Fund or Allot for the benefit of the Applicant's Spouse an amount of the Applicant's Benefits equal to an amount of the Splittable Contributions made by, for, or on behalf of the Applicant.
Splittable Contribution	Has the same meaning as in the SIS Regulations.
Spouse	Has the same meaning as in the SIS Act, however: (a) where a person has more than one Spouse, the Trustee may determine: (i) who is a Spouse for the purposes of this document; and (ii) the proportions a Benefit is payable to each Spouse if there is no BDBN; (b) the Trustee, in determining whether a relationship is on a genuine domestic basis, may have regard to any matters, and attach weight to these matters, as it determines;

Term	Definition
Spouse (continued)	(c) a person can be a Spouse of a Member even if that person or the Member is: (i) legally married to someone else; or (ii) the Spouse of another person.
Statutory Authority	Means a regulatory body or person having responsibility for the administration of superannuation.
Superannuation Death Benefit	Has the same meaning as in the Tax Act.
Superannuation Lump Sum	Has the same meaning as in the Tax Act.
Superannuation Member Benefit	Has the same meaning as in the Tax Act.
Tax	Includes any tax, surcharge, Levy, impost or duty payable by the Trustee.
Tax Act	Means the Income Tax Assessment Act 1936 (Cth) and the Income Tax Assessment Act 1997 (Cth) and any regulations or public rulings issued under those Acts.
Temporary Incapacity	Has the same meaning as in the SIS Act and SIS Regulations.
Trustee	Means: (a) as at the date of this document – SMSF Trustee Name; and (b) in all cases - the trustee or trustees for the time being of the Fund.
Unclaimed Benefits	Means those Benefits described as unclaimed money under the SIS Act.
Unrestricted Non-Preserved Amount	Means an amount determined in accordance with the SIS Regulations.

Review notes

1. Throughout the trust deed and schedules, there are a number of terms that are used on multiple occasions.
2. All of these terms are summarised in the above table.
3. Some terms are defined with reference to the Law.
4. If you are interested, contact the adviser that assisted you in setting up this SMSF and we can provide through them a separate table which summarises the definitions (extracted from the relevant legislation) as at the date of this document.

4 Rules

4.1 The Fund is governed by this document and the Law.

5 Structure

5.1 The Fund is established by, and starts on the date of, this document.

5.2 The Fund is at all times vested in the Trustee and managed by the Trustee upon the terms and subject to the trusts, powers, authorities and discretions in this document.

5.3 The Fund consists of all assets held by (or on account of) the Trustee upon the trusts of this document.

6 Covenants

6.1 The Trustee must act in accordance with this document and the Law.

6.2 If there is any inconsistency between this document and the Law, the provisions of the Law prevail.

7 Trustee

Purpose

7.1 Subject to the Law:

- **a** the Trustee must at all times be a Constitutional Corporation; or
- **b** if the Trustee is not a Constitutional Corporation, the sole or primary purpose of the Fund must be the provision of old-age pensions as that term is defined in the *Commonwealth of Australia Constitution Act*.

Self managed superannuation funds

7.2 A person can only be:

- **a** the Trustee; or
- **b** a Director of the Trustee (if the Trustee is a Constitutional Corporation), in accordance with the provisions of this clause.

7.3 Subject to this document, where the Fund has a sole Member, the Trustee must either be:

- **a** a Constitutional Corporation where the Member is:
  - (i) the sole Director; or
  - (ii) one of only two Directors, and the Member and the other Director are related; or
  - (iii) one of only two Directors, and the Member is not employed by the other Director; or
- **b** two Individual Trustees comprising the Member and another person who is either:
  - (i) related to the Member; or
  - (ii) not an Employer of the Member.

7.4 Subject to this document, where the Fund has more than one Member, the Trustee must satisfy one of the following, however no Member of the Fund may be employed by another Member of the Fund unless permitted by the Law:

- **a** a Constitutional Corporation where each Member is a Director and each Director is a Member; or
- **b** Individual Trustees where each Member is an Individual Trustee and each Individual Trustee is a Member of the Fund.

7.5 Regardless of any legislation regulating trusts in the jurisdiction of the situs of the Fund, and subject to this document:

- **a** a sole trustee may act; and
- **b** a retiring trustee is fully discharged, even where only one trustee remains after the retirement.

7.6 The requirements in this clause are subject to any other rules in the Law.

Appointment

7.7 Subject to the Law, the Members with the majority of Benefits in the Fund may at their sole discretion in writing:

a remove any Trustee of the Fund; or

b appoint a Trustee, with, or in replacement of, the existing Trustee.

7.8 The LPR of:

a a deceased Member;

b a Member who has lost legal capacity; or

c a Member who has appointed the LPR as the Member's attorney, may exercise that Member's power to appoint a Trustee.

7.9 Where a Member is under the age of 18 years, a parent or guardian of the Member may exercise that Member's power to appoint a Trustee.

7.10 If the Fund has no remaining Members and no other person mentioned in this clause has the power to appoint a Trustee, then the LPR of the last remaining Member to have an LPR may appoint a Trustee.

Ceasing to act

7.11 Subject to the Law, a Trustee ceases to act if:

a being an Individual, they die or otherwise lose legal capacity;

b being a Constitutional Corporation, it is placed into receivership or liquidation or an administrator is appointed;

c the Trustee is disqualified, removed or suspended from office under the Law;

d the Trustee resigns by notice to a majority of the Members; or

e the Trustee is removed from office by written notice given to the Trustee by Members with the majority of Benefits in the Fund.

Powers personal

7.12 Apart from the circumstances set out in this clause, the powers of the Trustee are personal to the persons nominated and cannot be exercised by any other person, entity or court.

Transfer of assets

7.13 On retirement or removal of a Trustee, the Trustee must:

- **a** hand over the books, accounts, documents and property of the Fund to the new trustee;
- **b** do everything necessary to vest the assets of the Fund in the new trustee;
- **c** do everything reasonably required by the new trustee to hand over to the new trustee possession and control of any assets registered with third parties;
- **d** do all other things reasonably required by the new trustee to inform the new trustee of the arrangements of the Fund.

Remuneration

7.14 If permitted by the Law, if any person acting as a Trustee is a trustee company, lawyer, financial adviser or accountant, that person (or any firm of which they are a member) may charge all usual and reasonable professional fees for professional work done in the administration of the Fund, regardless of whether the work performed is within the normal scope of the profession of which the Trustee is a member.

Members

7.15 No Individual Trustee, Director or officer of a Constitutional Corporation or Employee of an Employer is by virtue of their office or the powers delegated to them by the Trustee disqualified from being a Member of the Fund or from exercising rights or deriving any Benefits as a Member of the Fund.

8 Liability

8.1 A Trustee is not liable:

- **a** for the consequences of any act, omission, error or forgetfulness whether of law or fact on the part of the Trustee or their legal or other advisers; or
- **b** generally for any breach of duty or trust,
- **c** unless it is proved to have been committed, given or omitted in bad faith, recklessly or grossly negligently by that Trustee.

Indemnity

8.2 The Trustee is indemnified out of the Fund against liabilities incurred by it:

- **a** in the execution, or attempted execution, of this document;
- **b** because of the failure to exercise any of the trusts, authorities, powers or discretions of this document; or
- **c** by virtue of being the Trustee,
- **d** unless the loss or liability is proved to be caused by any act or omission or fraud or in bad faith, or the wilful misconduct, recklessness or gross negligence of the Trustee.

Review notes

1. The Law is prescriptive about how a superannuation fund satisfies the definition of being an SMSF.
2. The basic principle is that all Trustees (whether individuals or directors of a corporate Trustee) must be Members of the SMSF and vice versa.

3. There are exceptions to this rule. While there can be a mixture of individual and corporate Trustees, there must not be more than four Trustees in total.
4. Special rules also apply in relation to any Trustee who has lost capacity, is under the age of 18 or dies. Generally the LPR for the Member is permitted to act as Trustee on their behalf in these circumstances.
5. The Tax Office requires notification confirming the Trustee of an SMSF. The standard forms also require the Trustee to provide a number of declarations confirming its understanding of the Law.
6. In certain instances, particularly where an event of bankruptcy occurs, persons will be disqualified from acting as a Trustee of an SMSF, and again in this type of situation, specialist advice should be sought.

9 Members

9.1 The Trustee may, on the date and terms it determines, admit as a Member any person who applies, unless the admission would cause the Fund to breach the Law.

9.2 Each Member is deemed to have consented to be bound by this document.

10 Notification to Members

10.1 The Trustee must give all new Members a Disclosure Document containing the information as required by the Law.

10.2 The Trustee must annually give Members, former Members (or their LPR) and Beneficiaries any information required by the Law.

10.3 A copy of any documents required by the Law must be made available for inspection by any Member or Beneficiary on their request.

10.4 The Trustee must notify the Members of the manner, time and place in which meetings of the Members held under the Law and for the purposes of this document are to be held.

Review notes

1. While (in order to qualify as an SMSF) each Individual Trustee must be a Member and vice versa, there are still a number of notifications that must be provided to Members when they join an SMSF.
2. There must also be regular Trustee meetings, in particular whenever significant decisions or events relating to the Fund need to be made.
3. Where the Trustee is a company, all the rules that apply under the Corporations Act 2001 (Cth) in relation to conducting meetings and recording decisions must be followed.
4. There is no equivalent legislation for Individual Trustees, however a similar approach should still be adopted.
5. Generally each Trustee (or Director) will get one vote. In some situations, steps may be taken to change the voting ability of each Trustee to align with their respective Member balances of entitlements under the Fund, however specialist advice should be obtained before implementing this type of arrangement.

11 Ceasing to be a Member

11.1 A person ceases to be a Member on the first of the following to occur:

- **a** the Trustee determines that the Member has been paid all of their Benefit from the Fund;
- **b** where the Member dies, the Trustee determines that the deceased Member's Benefit has been paid in accordance with this document;
- **c** the Trustee determines that the Member's membership would cause the Fund to cease complying with the Law; or
- **d** the Trustee acting reasonably determines that the Member should cease to be a Member.

Review notes

1. There are a range of reasons that a Member may choose to leave a Fund, including:
   (a) a desire to become a member of another fund (including an industry fund);
   (b) due to the dissolution of a spousal relationship with another Member;
   (c) a decision to otherwise wind up the Fund;
   (d) the Member becomes a disqualified person.
2. Whenever a Member is seeking to withdraw their Benefits from the Fund, the Trustee is obliged to ensure that payments are done in a way that complies with the Law and that the transfer is completed in a timely manner.

12 Contributions

Eligibility

12.1 The Trustee may accept Contributions from a Member, an Employer or any other Permitted Entity.

Allocation

12.2 Each Contribution must be allocated within 28 days after the end of the month in which it is received.

Guarantee Act

12.3 Where the Trustee accepts Contributions under the Guarantee Act, the Trustee must give all certificates, reports and other information required by the Guarantee Act.

13 General Contribution provisions

Form

13.1 A Contribution may be made either:

a in cash; or

b by transfer of an asset or assets, if permitted by the Law.

Obligations

13.2 Subject to the Law:

a in the absence of any agreement to the contrary, no Member, Employer or Permitted Entity is obliged to make a Contribution in any Financial Year; and

b a person may remain a Member despite no Contributions being made in respect of that Member for any Financial Year.

Limits

13.3 The Trustee must refuse to accept any Contribution or Shortfall Component if:

a under the Law the Contribution is not authorised to be made;

b the Contribution is in excess of the amount of Contributions that can be made on the Member's behalf under the Law;

c acceptance of the Contribution or Shortfall Component would cause the Fund to no longer qualify as a Complying Superannuation Fund; or

d any Statutory Authority directs the Trustee not to accept a Contribution by an Employer or any Shortfall Component.

Eligibility

13.4 If any Contribution or Shortfall Component is accepted by the Fund in breach of the Law, the Trustee must refund the Contribution or Shortfall Component as required by the Law, less any:

a Tax payable that the Member has authorised the Trustee to pay;

b charge which an Insurer may have made; and

c reasonable costs.

Review notes

1. Subject to the rules in relation to transactions with Members and other related parties, the Trustee may accept cash or assets given to the Fund by way of Contributions.
2. Contributions can also be made via a roll-over or transfer from another superannuation fund, as long as the strict requirements of the Law are complied with.
3. The PDS sets out in detail the basis on which Contributions can be made for a Member.
4. The law in this area has changed regularly since 2000 and specialist advice should be obtained if there are any doubts about whether a Contribution will fall within the rules.
5. This can be particularly important where a Contribution may potentially be in excess of what is otherwise permitted under the Law, otherwise penalty tax rates can often apply.

14 Contribution splitting

Application

14.1 Subject to the Law, the Trustee may accept an application from an Applicant to Split the Applicant's Benefit (up to the Maximum Splittable Amount).

Split

14.2 If the Trustee accepts an application under this clause, the Trustee must effect the Split within 90 days after receiving the application, but cannot Allot any amount for the benefit of the Spouse unless they are a Member.

Review notes

1. Subject to the Law, the Trustee may permit Members to 'split' Contributions.
2. This means, for example, if one Member is receiving Contributions from, say, an employer, they can choose to have those Contributions directly allocated to, for example, their Spouse.
3. As with many other aspects of the Contribution rules, the exact requirements can be complex, and if there is any doubt about the ability to split the Contributions, specialist advice should be obtained.

15 Approved Benefit Arrangements

Asset transfers

15.1 Following a request of a Member, or the LPR of a Member, the Trustee may determine to Allot, transfer or rollover all or part of any Member's Account to any other Member's Account or Approved Benefit Arrangement, in accordance with the Law.

Effect

15.2 Once an Allotment, transfer or rollover under this clause has been effected:

a the receipt of the transferred or rolled over Benefit by the proper officer of the Approved Benefit Arrangement is a complete discharge to the Trustee and the Trustee has no responsibility to see to the application of it; and

b all the rights and interest of that Member under this document (and all the rights and interest of any person otherwise entitled to claim in respect of the Member or on the occurrence of any event or circumstances affecting the Member) in respect of the amount paid are entirely extinguished.

Eligible Rollover Funds

15.3 The Trustee may if permitted by the Law, and must if required by the Law, transfer a Member's Benefit to an Eligible Rollover Fund and must give any information to the trustee of the Eligible Rollover Fund at the times and in the manner required by the Law.

Review notes

1. As set out above, where a Member chooses (or is forced) to leave a Fund, the entitlements of the Member should be transferred to an 'Approved Benefit Arrangement'.
2. The rules set out under the Law confirm the requirements that a Trustee must satisfy when making any type of transfer for an exiting Member, and the Trustee must be satisfied that the Fund receiving the Member's Benefit does comply with all the aspects of the Law.
3. Best practice dictates that the Trustee should obtain a declaration from the trustee of the recipient fund that it does meet the relevant criteria.

16 Accumulation Account

16.1 The Trustee may establish an Accumulation Account for each Member or Beneficiary.

16.2 The Trustee may credit to and debit the Accumulation Account for a Member or Beneficiary any amounts required by this document and the Law as it determines.

17 Pension Account

17.1 The Trustee may establish a Pension Account in respect of a Pensioner.

17.2 The Trustee must transfer to the Pension Account for a Pensioner any assets of the Fund or amounts determined in accordance with this document which the Trustee determines necessary to cash the Member's Benefit as a Pension.

17.3 The Trustee may credit to the Pension Account for a Pensioner as it determines:

a the portion of the Earnings (if positive); and

b any other amounts that the Trustee determines and which are permitted by the Law.

17.4 The Trustee may debit to the Pension Account for a Pensioner all Benefits paid to the Pensioner.

18 Income Account

18.1 The Trustee must establish an Income Account for the Fund.

18.2 The Trustee must credit and debit the Income Account with all amounts required by this document and the Law.

18.3 At the end of each Financial Year or at any other time that the Trustee determines or the Law requires, the Trustee must determine:

a the Earnings in respect of the period since the previous determination; and

b the Fund Earning Rate.

18.4 Subject to this document and the Law, the Trustee must use the Fund Earning Rate to determine the proportion of the Earnings to be credited or debited to other Accounts (including Member Accounts, Pension Accounts or Reserve Accounts) from the Income Account.

18.5 The Trustee must, when required by the Statutory Authority or the Law, notify the Members of the basis of the calculation of the Fund Earning Rate.

19 Floating Account

Establishment

19.1 The Trustee may establish a Floating Account for the Fund.

Transfers

19.2 The Trustee must transfer to the credit of the Floating Account any amount remaining in the Income Account after distribution of Earnings.

Separation

19.3 Amounts credited to the Floating Account do not form part of any Member Account and any income earned by the Fund on the moneys held in the Floating Account must be credited to the Floating Account.

Use

19.4 The Floating Account may be used as the Trustee determines, including for the following purposes:

- **a** as part of a reserving strategy;
- **b** to supplement the Fund Earning Rate; and
- **c** to pay any Tax.

Adjustment of Member Account

19.5 The Trustee may adjust the credit of a Member Account to reflect the Fund Earning Rate applying at the date of payment.

20 Reserve Accounts

Establishment

20.1 Subject to the Law, the Trustee may establish one or more Reserve Accounts for the Fund and determine what amounts are credited or debited to those Accounts.

Investment strategy

20.2 The Trustee must formulate and implement a separate investment Strategy for any Reserve Account.

No entitlement

20.3 No Member, nor any other person, has any entitlement to any amount held in a Reserve Account.

Review notes

1. In order to give effect to the Fund's investment strategy and in turn discharge the obligations imposed by the sole purpose test (as explained in the PDS), there must be flexibility to deal with all assets of the Fund.
2. The primary tools available to the Trustee to do this are the various types of Accounts that they choose to establish within the Fund.
3. During the lifecycle of a Fund, the Trustee will generally establish most, if not all, of the following Accounts:
   (a) Accumulation Account – this manages the ongoing Contributions and investments of Members up until they reach a condition of release. Generally, there will be a separate Accumulation Account for each Member;
   (b) Pension Account – once a Member starts receiving an Income Stream, the Pension Account will be used to manage the Pension payments;
   (c) Income Account – this Account manages the return on investments, prior to them being allocated to another Account;
   (d) Floating Account – this Account is designed to receive any excess Earnings that are not otherwise allocated to a Member's Accumulation Account;
   (e) Reserve Account – Reserve Accounts, within strict parameters set by the Tax Office and the Law, can be used to help manage fluctuations in returns across the lifecycle of the Fund. Reserve accounts can also be used to help manage the payment of income streams, lump sum payments on death and managing allocation of Contributions;
   (f) whenever using a Reserve Account, the Trustee should set out the parameters of the Account as part of the investment strategy for the Fund.

21 Valuation of Fund

21.1 At the end of each Financial Year or at any other time the Trustee determines or the Law requires, the Trustee must:

- **a** make a valuation of all of the assets of the Fund;
- **b** transfer any surplus or deficiency in the valuation of assets, other than specific investments, to the Income Account; and
- **c** ensure that the records and accounts of the Fund reflect the valuation of each asset.

22 Records, reports and audit

Trustee obligations

22.1 The Trustee must:

- **a** keep accounts of all dealings of the Fund;
- **b** safely retain all documents for any period required by the Law;
- **c** prepare and lodge all documents required by the Law;
- **d** ensure the Fund is audited at the end of each Financial Year and that the Auditor provides any certificates required by the Statutory Authority;
- **e** once each Financial Year, report on the affairs of the Fund to the Members in the form required by the Law;
- **f** record against a Member's Benefit or Benefit Entitlement, a Payment Flag that has been validly served on the Trustee under the Law until it is validly lifted;
- **g** comply with any direction or requirement of the Statutory Authority or a court in relation to the Fund.

Review notes

1. While the Trustee may delegate a number of its duties, it is still ultimately responsible for the way in which the Fund is managed.
2. One important aspect of this is that all assets, agreements and transactions on behalf of the Fund should be recorded in the name of the Trustee.
3. The Trustee must also keep proper accounts for the Fund and determine the value of the Fund at least once a year.
4. The accounts must in turn be audited each year.

23 Service providers

23.1 The Trustee may determine to appoint any one or more persons, as:

- **a** investment manager;
- **b** actuary;
- **c** administration manager;
- **d** Auditor;
- **e** custodian; or
- **f** any other consultants the Trustee determines as appropriate for the Fund.

Review notes

1. Each Trustee is ultimately responsible for all aspects of the Fund.
2. The Trustee however is able to seek specialist advice, particularly in areas where they do not necessarily have skills or experience themselves.
3. Any delegation of various aspects of the Fund to one or more of the types of consultants or advisers outlined above is often appropriate.

24 Insurance

Member policies

24.1 The Trustee may effect Policies with an Insurer and may secure the Benefit of a Member via any form of Policy.

Member requests

24.2 Where a Member notifies the Trustee to effect a Policy of a specified type in respect of the Member, the Trustee must effect that Policy unless it would cause the Fund to cease being a Complying Superannuation Fund.

Review Notes

1. The Trustee can arrange for insurance in relation to each Member.
2. Any insurance arrangements should align with the overall investment strategy of the Fund.
3. Specialist advice should be obtained given the relatively complex rules in relation to insurance held via superannuation as well as related Tax consequences.
4. While generally the rules in relation to life insurance are simple, particularly where cover for total and permanent disablement, trauma or salary continuance are desired, there are a number of restrictions that need to be considered.
5. Similarly, while an SMSF is permitted to self-insure against various risks, specialist advice should be obtained before doing so.

25 Tax

25.1 The Trustee may deduct Tax from any Benefit payable to a Beneficiary in relation to a Contribution or Shortfall Component before the Contribution or Shortfall Component is credited to the Accumulation Account of a Member.

Review notes

1. There are a significant number of taxes that can apply to an SMSF, including:
   (a) income tax;
   (b) capital gains tax;
   (c) contributions tax;
   (d) various surcharges;
   (e) stamp duty; and
   (f) land tax.
2. Generally, Earnings that relate to a Pension Account will be tax free.
3. Similarly, the payment of a death benefit to people who satisfy the definition of a 'tax dependant' will also be tax free.
4. The rules about taxation and SMSFs are relatively complex and change regularly, so specialist advice should be obtained.

26 Types of Benefits

Entitlement

26.1 Where a Member becomes entitled to a Benefit under this document and the Law, and there are no cashing restrictions that apply to the Benefit under the Law, the Member may elect by notice to the Trustee to be paid the Benefit in one or more of the forms permitted by the Law, including:

a one or more Superannuation Lump Sums; or

b one or more Income Streams.

Pre 1 July 2007 entitlements

26.2 Where a Member was already receiving one or more Income Streams before 1 July 2007, that Member may continue to receive them, as permitted by the Law.

Election

26.3 Unless the Trustee otherwise determines, an election given by a Member under this document:

a is not binding on the Trustee;

b is to be provided before the Benefit starts to be paid; and

c must confirm the amount to be paid and the extent to which the amount is to be paid as any one or more types of Benefit.

Restrictions

26.4 The Trustee may only pay a Benefit in accordance with any cashing restrictions imposed by the Law.

Transfers

26.5 Where a Member or a Beneficiary is entitled to be paid a Benefit, the Trustee may transfer any:

a interest in a Policy to the Member or Beneficiary;

b assets of the Fund of an equivalent value to that Member or Beneficiary.

Review notes

1. There are two ways that a Member can access their entitlements in an SMSF, namely:
   (a) lump sum; and
   (b) Income Stream.
2. The Trustee determines how Benefits are paid, and can combine one or more lump sums with one or more Income Streams.
3. Importantly, the entitlement to Benefits is subject to the various expenses of the Fund, which must be deducted before Benefits are paid.

27 Preservation

27.1 The Trustee must Preserve the amounts of Contributions as required by the Law.

28 Payment of Unrestricted Non-Preserved Amount

28.1 Subject to the Law:

- **a** a Member may elect at any time to withdraw all or any part of their Unrestricted Non-Preserved Amount by giving notice to the Trustee; and
- **b** the minimum Unrestricted Non-Preserved Amount which may be withdrawn by a Member must be determined by the Trustee and notified to the relevant Members.

29 Additional benefits

29.1 The Trustee may determine to pay to a Member's Accumulation Account:

- **a** an Anti-detriment Payment;
- **b** any portion of the Floating Account; and
- **c** any other amounts allowed under the Law.

30 Retention

30.1 Where a Member or Beneficiary does not require Benefits to be paid, the Trustee may retain all or any part of any Benefit in the Fund until the earlier of:

a the date the Member or Beneficiary entitled to the Benefit notifies the Trustee that it requires the Benefit; or

b the date the Benefit is required to be paid under the Law or this document.

31 Compulsory payment

Payment

31.1 The Trustee must cash a Member's Benefit as soon as practicable after the first of the following:

a the death of a Member; or

b as required under this document; or

c as required under the Law.

Cashing

31.2 The Trustee may cash a Member's Benefit in any one or more of the following ways:

a a single lump sum;

b an interim lump sum and a final lump sum;

c one or more Pensions; and

d one or more Annuities.

32 Voluntary payment

32.1 Subject to the Law, any Member may elect to receive a Benefit on or after the occurrence to them of any of the following events:

a Retires from Gainful Employment;

b suffers Permanent Incapacity;

c suffers Temporary Incapacity;

d if a temporary resident, departs Australia permanently in circumstances described in the Law, and requests the Trustee for the release of their Benefits;

e ends Gainful Employment with an Employer who had (at any time) made Contributions to the Fund;

f suffers Severe Financial Hardship;

g attains age 65;

h suffers events that lend to release on Compassionate Grounds as determined by the Trustee;

i attains Preservation Age; or

j satisfies any other condition of release permitted by the Law.

Review notes

1. As outlined above, there are various triggers for the voluntary payment of a Benefit as well as the mandatory or compulsory triggers, such as death.
2. There are a number of rules in relation to the steps the Trustee must follow when paying Benefits following death.
3. In relation to the voluntary triggers, the Trustee, working with the Member, has more discretion as to whether any Benefits will be released, and if so, the basis on which to do so.

33 Pension Benefits

33.1 Subject to the Law and this document, the following provisions apply to the payment of a Pension by the Trustee:

a any Pension must be cashed in accordance with any Trustee resolutions or pension agreement;

b if the amount standing to the credit of the relevant Pension Account is less than the instalment to be cashed, the lesser amount must be paid and the Trustee's liability in respect of the cashing of the Pension is discharged;

c an amount representing the capital value of a Benefit may be applied to the purchase of an Annuity in the Trustee's name and payments under that Annuity to be made directly to the Member; and

d if a Pensioner:

(i) commits an act of bankruptcy; or
(ii) becomes or is insolvent or enters into any deed of assignment or deed of arrangement,

then the Pension immediately ceases and the Pension Account becomes an Accumulation Account, provided the cessation of the Pension is not prohibited under the Law.

34 Unclaimed Benefits

34.1 As required by the Law, the Trustee must:

a give to the Statutory Authority a statement of Unclaimed Benefits; and

b pay any Unclaimed Benefits to the Statutory Authority.

35 Forfeited Benefits

Forfeiture

35.1 Subject to the Law, Benefits retained by or payable out of the Fund must be forfeited and applied as the Trustee determines if:

a without the prior approval of the Trustee, the Member or Beneficiary purports to assign, alienate or charge any Benefits;

b the Member's interest in any Benefit becomes payable to or vested in any other person, company, government or other public authority;

c the Member is unable personally to receive or enjoy the whole or any portion of a Benefit;

d the Trustee determines the Member is incapable of managing their affairs; or e the Trustee determines the Member has committed a fraud or is guilty of dishonesty or embezzlement.

Establishment

35.2 The Trustee may establish a Forfeiture Account and may transfer to it any amounts forfeited under this document.

Treatment

35.3 Moneys held in the Forfeiture Account do not form part of any other Account and any income derived by the Fund in respect of moneys held in the Forfeiture Account must be credited to the Forfeiture Account.

Unclaimed Benefits

35.4 Subject to the Law, the Trustee may determine to treat as unclaimed, forfeit and transfer to an account for Unclaimed Benefits, any moneys in the Fund standing to the credit of any Member whose whereabouts are unknown.

Review notes

1. The circumstances where a Member's interest in an SMSF may be forfeited are relatively narrow.
2. Due to the seriousness of the consequences of forfeiting a Member's Benefit, the Trustee should obtain specialist advice before doing so.
3. Practically, the issue of forfeiture comes up most regularly in the context of a Member committing an act of bankruptcy.
4. This said, due to changes to the bankruptcy rules in the mid 2000s, a Member's entitlement in the Fund, while they remain in accumulation mode, will generally be protected on bankruptcy, with no dollar limit to this level of protection.

36 Death benefits

Payment if BDBN

36.1 If a Member has made a BDBN that at the date of their death is valid, any Benefit payable on or following the death of the Member must be paid by the Trustee as set out in the BDBN.

Payment if no BDBN

36.2 If a Member has not made a valid BDBN at the date of their death, the Trustee may determine how to pay the Member's Benefit.

Commutation

36.3 Subject to the Law, the Trustee may, and must where required by the Law:

- **a** discharge its liability to a Member or Beneficiary in respect of a Pension by paying to the Member or Beneficiary a Superannuation Lump Sum equal to the balance of the relevant Pension in the Pension Account; or
- **b** determine that the commutation of a Pension Benefit following the death of a Pensioner is treated as a Superannuation Member Benefit or a Superannuation Death Benefit.

Review notes

1. The death of a Member triggers a compulsory cashing obligation.
2. This means the Trustee must either pay a lump sum or Income Stream in accordance with the Law.
3. The payment must be to a 'dependant', which broadly includes only immediate family members or the LPR of the Member (so it can then be distributed in accordance with the Member's will).
4. Where the Benefit is paid to a non-tax dependant (tax dependants are essentially only a spouse or a child under the age of 18), additional tax may be payable.
5. There is the ability for the Trustee to make a payment in excess of the Member's balance using the 'anti detriment' provisions under the Tax Act. Specialist advice should be obtained before the Trustee makes any form of death benefit payment, particularly if the anti-detriment provisions may be applicable.
6. The Trustee must also take into account the impact of any nominations (these are explained in more detail below).

37 BDBNs

Non-BDBN

37.1 A Member may at any time make a Non-BDBN designating one or more Nominated Beneficiaries of any Benefit payable by the Trustee on or following the death of the Member, however the notice:

a must be provided to the Trustee; and

b is not binding on the Trustee.

BDBN

37.2 A Member may at any time provide notice to the Trustee

that they have made a BDBN if the BDBN:

a is in writing;

b is signed and dated by the Member in the presence of two witnesses, who:

(i) have both turned 18 years; and

(ii) are not a Nominated Beneficiary; and

c contains a declaration signed and dated by the witnesses, stating that the notice was signed by them both and the Member while all together.

37.3 A Member may in a BDBN nominate:

a the proportions in which the Benefit is to be paid to each Nominated Beneficiary; and

b the manner or form (whether by way of Pension, Superannuation Lump Sum or otherwise) in which those Benefits must be paid.

37.4 A BDBN may be confirmed, amended or revoked at any time by the Member however will be otherwise effective until revoked.

37.5 A BDBN may only be revoked by:

a making a later valid BDBN; or

b written notice to the Trustee.

37.6 Where:

a a Member makes a BDBN that is otherwise valid; and

b the BDBN contains a nomination in favour of a person who is deceased at the date a payment is to be made,

the BDBN will be invalid in relation to of the nomination in favour of that deceased person and the Trustee must:

c pay the Member's Benefit in accordance with the remaining terms of the BDBN; or

d if no other person is validly nominated, pay the Member's Benefit as if the BDBN was invalid at the date of the Member's death.

38 Payment if no BDBN

38.1 Subject to this document and the Law, any Benefit payable on the death of a Member may be paid or applied however the Trustee determines, in the proportions the Trustee decides to any one or more of a Member's:

a Nominated Beneficiaries (if any) designated in a Non-BDBN;
b Dependants; or
c LPR.

39 Payment if BDBN is invalid or ineffective

39.1 Subject to the Law, if a Member makes a BDBN that at the date of death is invalid or ineffective, the BDBN is treated as a Non-BDBN, deemed to be dated the day of the purported BDBN.

40 Payment where conflicting instructions

40.1 If a Member has:

a validly made a BDBN or a Non-BDBN or both; and
b validly nominated a Reversionary Beneficiary in respect of their Benefit,
c then the nomination of the Reversionary Beneficiary must be followed by the Trustee, regardless of any BDBN or Non-BDBN.

Review notes

1. There are essentially six possible scenarios in relation to any death benefit payment and these are summarised below.
   (a) No nomination - the Member may have made no direction or nomination to the Trustee. In this situation, the Trustee has complete discretion as to how to distribute the death benefit payment.
   (b) Non-BDBN - if the Member has made a nomination which does not satisfy the requirements of a BDBN, the Trustee retains complete discretion as to how to distribute the death benefit, although it should still take into account what is set out in the Non-BDBN.
   (c) Lapsing BDBN - where there is a valid BDBN, the Trustee must pay the death benefit in accordance with it. The only situation where the Trustee need not follow the lapsing BDBN is where, even though it is otherwise validly prepared, it is stated to be enforceable for a defined period (often three years). If the Member dies outside the relevant period, then the Trustee is not bound to follow the BDBN.
   (d) Non lapsing BDBN - it is possible for Members to create BDBNs that are non-lapsing. If they are validly prepared, they are binding on the Trustee.
   (e) Hardwired BDBN - BDBNs can be embedded (or hardwired) into the trust deed. Specialist advice should be obtained in relation to this approach, which is generally adopted where there are concerns that a nomination, even if otherwise a valid BDBN, may not be followed.
   (f) Reversionary Beneficiary - where a Member has been receiving an Income Stream, it is possible to establish that Income Stream in a way that it automatically reverts or passes to another person, regardless of any nomination that may have been made.

2. The interplay between death benefit payments and a Member's estate plan can be complex and best practice dictates that Members should implement a comprehensive estate plan and complementary strategy in relation to their superannuation entitlements (sometimes referred to as an 'SMSF will').
3. Furthermore, the impact of incapacity should also be considered. For example, if a lapsing BDBN is to be implemented, thought should be given to allowing the LPR of a Member who is incapacitated to have the power to sign an updated BDBN on their behalf.

Information to be provided

40.2 If a Member's Benefit or Benefit Entitlement becomes subject to a Payment Split, the Trustee must give the Member and the Non-Member Spouse all material required by the Law.

Trustee may create new interest

40.3 Subject to the Law, the Trustee may admit a Non-Member Spouse in respect of a Payment Split as a Member if the Non-Member Spouse requests the Trustee to do so.

40.4 If the Trustee admits a Non-Member Spouse as a Member, the Trustee must reduce the Member's Benefit Entitlement in respect of the Payment Split by the amount required by the Law.

Interest of Non-Member Spouse

40.5 If a Non-Member Spouse in respect of a Payment Split is not a Member, the Trustee must:

a either:
  - (i) transfer the entitlement of the Non-Member Spouse to an Approved Benefit Arrangement; or
  - (ii) pay the entitlement of the Non-Member Spouse to the Non-Member Spouse; and

- **b** reduce the Member's Benefit Entitlement in respect of the Payment Split by the amount required by Law.

40.6 Any payment, transfer or rollover of the entitlement of a Non-Member Spouse in accordance with a Payment Split is a complete discharge to the Trustee.

40.7 The Trustee may deduct from the amount to be paid in respect of a Payment Split any Tax that is calculated by the Trustee to be payable.

41 Family Law fees

41.1 The Trustee may:

- **a** charge reasonable fees in respect of any action taken by the Trustee under the *Family Law Act 1975* (Cth); and
- **b** determine to recoup any such fees from:
  - (i) a Member's Benefit Entitlement; or
  - (ii) the entitlements of the Non-Member Spouse.

Review notes

1. Where a Member of the Fund has a relationship breakdown with a Spouse, there are provisions under government legislation that can require a Member's interest in the Fund to be 'split' with their former Spouse.
2. Where these rules apply, the Trustee can be required to reallocate entitlements within the Fund and often will be required to then transfer the entitlement to another fund.
3. As with a number of other aspects of SMSFs, where a Payment Split is to take place, specialist advice should normally be obtained, primarily because of the number of different laws that can apply (for example, tax, superannuation, family law and stamp duty).

42 Amendment

42.1 Subject to this document and the Law, the Trustee may

amend, alter, vary or absolutely revoke or resettle all or any of the provisions set out in this document, including any schedules, with immediate, prospective or retrospective effect.

Limitation

42.2 No amendment may be made that would:

- **a** cause the trusts to fail by reason of the rule against perpetuities, unless otherwise permitted by law;
- **b** allow a person other than a Constitutional Corporation to be a Trustee, unless the governing rules at all times provide that the sole or primary purpose of the Fund is the provision of old-age pensions;
- **c** cause a BDBN made by a Member to become invalid or ineffective without the written consent of that Member or their LPR; or
- **d** cause a BDBN made by a Member to become invalid or ineffective after the date of that Member's death.

43 Termination

Events

43.1 The trusts terminate and the Fund is wound up if any of the following events happen:

- **a** all Members agree to terminate the Fund;
- **b** the Trustee determines to terminate the Fund; or
- **c** the Fund is required by Law to be terminated.

Notice

43.2 Upon the trusts terminating, the Trustee must give notice to the Members of the Closing Date.

43.3 From the Closing Date no further Contribution may be made by any Employer or any Member, other than arrears of Contributions due on or before the Closing Date.

Surplus

43.4 If a surplus remains after paying all Benefits for Members and Beneficiaries, that surplus must, subject to the requirements of the Law and this document, be paid by the Trustee as it determines.

Payment to other persons

43.5 If any payment of Benefits under this clause is required by the Law to be deferred until the occurrence of a specified event, then the Member is not entitled to receive that Benefit and the Trustee may determine to:

- **a** transfer the Benefit to another Complying Superannuation Fund;
- **b** purchase an Annuity or Pension with the Benefits commencing no earlier than the specified event; or
- **c** transfer the Benefits to an Approved Deposit Fund.

Review notes

1. The requirements under the Law in relation to the winding up of the Fund are detailed and must be followed by the Trustee precisely.
2. For most SMSFs, the winding up event will be triggered by the death of the last remaining Member.
3. In this scenario, it will generally be the LPR of that Member who has the responsibility for winding up the Fund.
4. Often that Member will not have had any particular involvement with the Fund historically, and indeed, may have no prior experience in relation to SMSFs.
5. Seeking appropriate specialist advice is often critical in the context of the winding up of an SMSF.

44 Powers

44.1 In addition to all powers at law, the Trustee has the powers listed at Schedule 1.

45 Governing jurisdiction

45.1 The governing jurisdiction is «Jurisdiction Law MC».

45.2 The situs of the Fund is deemed to be «Jurisdiction Law MC». However the Trustee may at any time determine by resolution that this settlement takes effect and that the administration of the Fund is to be in accordance with the laws of the state, territory or country in which the Trustee is domiciled, resident or has a place of business.

46 Interpretation

46.1 In this document:

- **a** singular words include the plural, and vice versa;
- **b** each word suggesting a gender includes all other genders, including neutral gender;
- **c** a reference to a person includes natural persons, firms, companies and any form of a corporation, trustee, trust, partnership, associations, unincorporated body, government and local authority or agency, or any other entity whether or not it comprises a separate legal entity;
- **d** a reference to a clause, schedule or annexure are references to this document and references to this document include every clause, the matters set out in the Overview and any schedules or annexures;
- **e** if any person signs this document on behalf of a party pursuant to a power of attorney, they confirm that there is nothing that impacts on their authority to do so;
- **f** a reference to a document or agreement (including a reference to this document) means that entire document or agreement (including all schedules or annexures) as amended, supplemented, novated, varied or replaced;
- **g** a reference to a person includes that person's estate successors, legal personal representatives, executors, administrators, permitted substitutes and permitted assigns;
- **h** where any word or phrase is defined in this document, its other grammatical forms have a corresponding meaning;

i a reference to this document includes the agreement recorded by this document;

j headings and any table of contents are not to be taken into account in the construction of this document;

k a reference to legislation or to a modified, rewritten, consolidated provision or section of legislation (including subordinate legislation) is to that legislation as amended, re-enacted or replaced, and includes any subordinate legislation issued under it;

l the applicable time zone for any action required under this document is the one applying in the situs of the person responsible for performing the action;

m a reference to writing includes printing, typing, copying, facsimile, and any other method of representing words, symbols, figures or drawings in a visible and tangible manner or electronically;

n if any part of this document is illegal or unenforceable it can be severed, with the remaining clauses (or parts of the clause) remaining in force;

o if any part of this document is illegal or unenforceable in any jurisdiction, it can be severed in the relevant jurisdiction, with the remaining clauses (or parts of the clause) remaining in force;

p unless this document provides for a notice or communication to be given orally, any notice or other communication must be in writing and signed by the person giving the notice and be addressed to the address of the person to whom it is to be given;

q a reference to 'month' means a calendar month; and

r if any provision of this document is ambiguous, it is to be interpreted broadly to widen and not restrict the provisions.

Notices

46.2 A notice or other communication is deemed to be received:

a in the case of a posted letter, on the second Business Day after posting;

b in the case of delivery by generally recognised overnight courier, on the next Business Day after dispatch with that courier;

c in the case of personal delivery, on the date of delivery;

d in the case of facsimile transmission, at the time recorded on the transmission report from the machine from which the facsimile was sent; and

e in the case of transmission by email, on the day of transmission if there is confirmation that the transmission was completed before 5.00pm on a Business Day, and alternatively, on the next Business Day. Email service is effective only if there is confirmation that it was sent in full and without error and the message is not rejected or undeliverable as evidenced by a message to that effect received by the sender.

Counterparts

46.3 This document may be signed in any number of counterparts and all counterparts together make one document.

Schedule 1 - Powers of Trustee

Investment strategy

A The Trustee must formulate and give effect to one or more investment strategies having regard to the Fund's circumstances and the Law.

Specific investments

B The Trustee may determine to make separate investments in respect of certain Members or Beneficiaries (or certain classes of Members or Beneficiaries) of the Fund or in respect of different classes of investment for certain Members or Beneficiaries and if it does must:

(1) record who the investments are made for, for the purposes of determining allocations to the Member Account;

(2) credit the Member Account with any income and profit and debit it with any costs, charges or Tax in the proportions determined applicable.

General powers

C The Trustee may determine to:

(1) pay Benefits out of the Fund to a Member or a Dependant;

(2) decide who are Dependants for the purposes of this document;

(3) in case of the mental or physical ill health or incapacity of any person entitled to Benefits, pay or apply those Benefits or any part as the Trustee determines to or for the benefit of any person without being responsible for seeing to their application;

(4) undertake any step to commit the Trustee to conduct the Fund at all times as a Complying Superannuation Fund;
(5) seek modifications of or exemptions from the application of the Law to the Fund; and
(6) accept Contributions and any Shortfall Component from any person authorised to make Contributions or pay the Shortfall Component.

Other powers

The Trustee may:

Generally deal with Fund

(1) sell, call in, convert into money, grant options or rights to purchase, mortgage, charge, sub-charge, grant security interests in, carry on business, or otherwise deal with, dispose of or transfer any item or asset comprising the whole or part of the Fund or otherwise held by the Trustee under the terms of the Fund:
  a for such consideration; and
  b on such terms as in its discretion it may think fit as if it were the absolute and beneficial owner of the Fund;

Discretion

(2) allow all or any part of the Fund to be invested as authorised by this document;
(3) invest or reinvest in any form of investment:
  a authorised by law or not;
  b with or without disclosing the Fund; and
  c whether alone, jointly or in partnership with others including with the Trustee acting in any capacity;
(4) postpone the sale, calling in, realisation or conversion for any period, even if the asset is wasting, speculative or reversionary in nature;
(5) vary or transpose investments;

Forms of investment

(6) invest in any manner the Trustee determines, for example:
- **a** Property;
- **b** syndicates of any kind;
- **c** crowd sourced funding;
- **d** bank accounts and investments;
- **e** debentures and unsecured notes;
- **f** insurance bonds;
- **g** shares, units and convertible notes;
- **h** franchises;
- **i** government securities; or
- **j** common fund investments;

Power to lend

(7) lend moneys forming part of the Fund, or give credit to any person or company (including any company any Beneficiary may own shares in or is a director of) on such terms as the Trustee may decide:
- **a** at call or for a period of time;
- **b** at a rate of interest or at no interest; and
- **c** with the taking of security in any form or without security;

Power to borrow and to provide security

(8) raise or borrow moneys either alone or jointly with another or others, from any person including a firm or company, either bearing or free of interest and on terms and for purposes as the Trustee may decide;

(9) secure the repayment of any moneys or other indebtedness by mortgage, charge or other security or encumbrance over the whole or part of the Fund as the Trustee may decide;

Property

(10) hold, use or buy;

(11) construct, demolish, maintain, repair, renovate, recon-

struct, erect, develop or improve;

(12) sell, transfer or convey (including by auction, contract, tender or option);

(13) manage, hire, surrender, let, licence or lease on any terms all or any part of the Property (including, for example, for a period of more than 21 years);

(14) receive livestock on agistment;

(15) buy stock, plant, equipment and fittings;

(16) make allowances to and arrangements with tenants, including where a tenant is a Beneficiary;

(17) take on lease or exchange;

(18) take or grant options or rights in, including easements or any other right;

(19) exchange for other Property, either with or without consideration;

(20) alienate, mortgage, charge or pledge;

(21) allow any Beneficiary to occupy, utilise or have custody on whatever terms the Trustee determines, including free of any charge or only requiring reimbursement of expenses;

(22) reconvey, release or discharge, or otherwise deal with any Property;

(23) apply for, buy or otherwise acquire any patents, patent rights, copyrights, designs, trademarks, formulas, licences, concessions and anything else conferring exclusive, non-exclusive or limited rights to use any secret or other information about any invention:

(24) may be capable of being used for any of the purposes of the Fund; or

a the acquisition of which may benefit the Fund;

b use, exercise, develop or grant licences in respect of or otherwise turn to account any property rights or information acquired;

(25) co-own with any other person, to any degree and on any terms,any Property;

Commercial bills

(26) draw, endorse, accept, guarantee or be a party in any way to a commercial bill or other bill of exchange, promissory

note, letter of credit, hypothecation or other facility involving the raising, borrowing or lending of moneys by or to the Trustee;

Open bank accounts

(27) open any account with any bank or other financial institution for any of the purposes and deposit money in, withdraw money from and operate the account;

(28) authorise other persons to operate an account or sign any of the instruments set out above;

Attorney

(29) appoint any person as the representative or attorney of the Trustee for the purpose of executing any document which the Trustee is permitted or authorised to execute by this document or by law and to revoke any appointment;

Record and value assets

(30) record as an asset in the books of the Fund any identifiable Property, interest, right or benefit relating to the Fund, regardless of whether it would be recognised as an asset at law or under any relevant accounting standards.

(31) allocate a value to any identifiable Property, interest, right or benefit recorded as an asset in the books of the Fund;

Delegate

(32) authorise any person to act as its agent, attorney or delegate to hold any investment being part of the Fund as custodian and to perform any act or exercise any discretion within the Trustee's power including the power to appoint in turn its own agent, attorney or delegate. The appointment may be in respect of more than one delegate or severally and may include provisions to protect those dealing with the agent, attorney or delegate;

Guarantees and indemnities

(33) guarantee, indemnify, secure by way of mortgage, charge or otherwise over the whole or part of the Fund or undertake in any way the payment or repayment of money or debts (including any interest whether existing or to accrue) previously or then lent or to be advanced or any existing or future duties, undertakings, liabilities or obligations incurred or which may at any future time be incurred by any person whether a Beneficiary or not and to guarantee, indemnify or secure, with or without security, the due performance of any contract, agreement, covenant or obligation of any person whether a Beneficiary or not, either with or without security and either alone, jointly, severally or jointly and severally;

Agree and settle accounts

(34) agree and settle accounts with all persons (including the Trustee) liable to account with the Trustee about the Fund;

(35) sign effectual receipts, releases and discharges;

Insurance

(36) buy or acquire (with or without any options, rights, benefits, conditions or provisions):

- **a** any reversionary, deferred proprietary or other rights; or
- **b** any life, life endowment, sinking fund, term or other policy of insurance or assurance of any nature;

(37) pay any amount payable, for premiums or otherwise:

- **a** to effect or maintain any policy of insurance or assurance (whether or not owned by the Trustee); or
- **b** for the exercise or enjoyment of any option, right or benefit under any policy,

and the surrender of any policy for all purposes may be deemed by the Trustee to be a sale of the policy;

(38) if it is necessary to make any claim under a policy, do all things and sign all documents for the perfection or enforcement of any rights arising from or in connection with any policy;

Lease or hire

(39) take on lease, hire purchase, or in exchange, and enter into leasing agreements and hire purchase agreements in relation to, using money of the Fund or any Property as it determines;

(40) sign a surrender of lease of any Property with or without consideration;

Share acquisition

(41) enter into any contract, agreement or arrangement for the subscription, allotment, issue, purchase or acquisition of shares or other securities of any company or trust registered anywhere in the world;

(42) agree to or concur in any amendment or variation to the constitution or any scheme of arrangement of any company or trust;

Conflicts of interest

(43) exercise or concur in exercising all powers and discretions given under this document or by law notwithstanding that:

a it, or any person being a director or shareholder of the Trustee has or may have a direct or indirect interest in the mode or result of exercising the power or discretion or may benefit either directly or indirectly as a result of the exercise of the power or discretion; and

b the Trustee for the time being is the sole trustee;

Decide action

(44) decide or refer to an appropriate court, tribunal, arbitrator or mediator any action, proceeding, dispute, claim or

demand;

(45) settle all claims or accounts relating to the Fund;

(46) sign releases and do all things determined as appropriate;

Carry on business

(47) carry on any business, either alone or in partnership, with the same powers as if the business belonged to the Trustee absolutely;

(48) enter into, vary or terminate any partnership or profit sharing or other similar arrangement with any Trustee in their own capacity or any other capacity, and with or without any other person;

(49) operate any bank account opened by or on behalf of any business in which the Trustee is concerned or interested;

Establish and support a related entity

(50) establish and support out of the Fund any company, association, institution or other fund (including a superannuation fund) designed in any way to benefit:

- **a** any Beneficiary; or
- **b** the employees or ex-employees of any company, partnership, association or syndicate in which the Fund may have invested;

(51) grant pensions and allowances;

Power to appropriate Fund in specie

(52) appropriate in specie any portion of the Fund, or any investment to or towards the share or entitlement of a Beneficiary and to charge the share or entitlement with a sum of money by way of equality as the Trustee may think fit and for these purposes the Trustee may fix the value of any Property forming part of the Fund and the appropriation, charge and valuation will be binding on all persons who may at any time be entitled to any interest in the Fund;

Pay expenses

(53) pay out of the Fund all costs, charges and expenses incidental to the:

a management of the Fund;

b exercise of any power, authority or discretion; or

c carrying out or performing the role of Trustee of the Fund, which the Trustee incurs in any part of the world, including without limitation all:

d taxes in respect of the Fund;

e liabilities incurred in carrying on any business or owning any Property;

f costs in any way connected with the Fund; and

g amounts by way of penalty, settlement, probate, estate gift, stamp or revenue duty;

Employ

(54) employ any person (including any Beneficiary or the Trustee) in connection with any activities of the Trustee or in connection with anything required to be done under this document;

(55) determine the remuneration to be allowed and paid in respect of any employee;

(56) create or arrange any scheme of superannuation or similar arrangements for the benefit of any employee;

(57) act personally and charge and be paid from the Fund a reasonable remuneration;

(58) instead of acting personally, employ at the expense of the Fund any agents, managers, advisers and accountants (including any Beneficiary);

Trustee's power to deal with itself

(59) notwithstanding any rule of law to the contrary, to acquire for the Fund any Property the beneficial interest in which is at the date of acquisition the absolute property of the Trustee in its own right or as trustee of another fund

provided that any Property so acquired is acquired for a consideration being not greater than the current market value of the Property and upon acquisition the beneficial interest in the Property will be held by the Trustee upon the trusts contained in this document;

Protection

(60) take any action for the adequate protection of the Fund;

(61) take and act upon the opinion of any lawyer practising in any jurisdiction where the Fund or any part of it is invested:

- a about the status or the administration of the Fund; and
- b without being liable to any person for any act done by the Trustee consistent with that opinion (although nothing in this clause prevents the Trustee or any Beneficiary from applying to any court);

(62) do all other things incidental to the exercise of the powers and authorities conferred on the Trustee;

Elections

(63) access any concessions, exemptions, roll-overs or other relief that may be available in relation to any duty, costs or tax payable in respect of the Fund, including by making any elections or choices available under the Tax Act. For clarity, this includes making (without limitation) any elections or choices involving family trust elections, interposed entity elections and capital gains tax roll-over choices or elections;

Release of powers

(64) by revocable or irrevocable deed renounce and release any power conferred on the Trustee under the Fund in respect of the whole or part of the Fund or the income and upon the renunciation and release coming into effect, the power is to be taken to be at an end and no longer exercisable by the Trustee to the extent of the renunciation and release;

Merger

(65) concur in the merger or takeover of any company or trust in which shares or other securities forming part of the Fund are held;
(66) to exercise any rights attaching to shares or units in any company or trust held by the Trustee;
(67) otherwise consent to or take part in any corporate action;

Nominee

(68) allow any asset of the Fund to be held or registered in the name of any nominee or agent;
(69) deposit securities over or titles in the Property of the Fund with any bank or other lender or guarantor;

Directorships

(70) become a director of any company in which any moneys forming part of the Fund are from time to time invested and receive the remuneration attached to the office without being liable to account.

Review notes

1. As can be seen, the Trustee has extremely wide powers and discretions to invest the assets of the Fund as deemed fit.
2. There are however a number of limitations, and the key ones are set out below.
3. The Trustee must always act in what would be objectively considered prudent in the context of each situation.
4. An important benchmark as to whether the Trustee has acted prudently will be whether a decision was appropriate in the context of the Fund's investment strategy.
5. There is an obligation on the Trustee to have a formal written investment strategy that is current at all times.

6. The Trustee must also ensure it complies with the 'sole purpose test'. This test requires that all arrangements of the Fund are focused on providing retirement benefits for the Members.
7. In this regard, there are restrictions on the ability of an SMSF to borrow money (there are a few exceptions to this limitation, particularly in relation to limited recourse loan arrangements).
8. Further, SMSFs should ensure that all transactions are conducted on an arm's length basis.
9. There are also prohibitions in relation to 'in-house' assets. An in-house asset is an investment in or a loan to a related party.
10. The Trustee must ensure that at all times the market value of any in-house asset is less than 5% of the total market value of all assets of the Fund.
11. Finally, there is a prohibition on an SMSF acquiring assets from a Member or a related party of a Member unless the relevant asset is:
    (a) listed shares;
    (b) business real property (as defined by the Law);
    (c) a widely held unit trust; or
    (d) a unit trust, which although not widely held, has no debt.
12. Separately, a Trustee will be indemnified in relation to any action against it, so long as they were appropriately acting in their role as Trustee.

Appendix Two

TEMPLATE INVESTMENT STRATEGY

Template Investment Strategy

User Note: All aspects of this document needs to be reviewed and amended to reflect the circumstances of the Fund. Particular attention is needed in relation to items marked '#'. This document is a template only and specialist advice should be obtained before it is relied on.

1 Overview

Fund Profile

1.1 The [#insert] Superannuation Fund (Fund) is an allocated accumulation fund established on to provide lump sum retirement benefits for members as well as death/disablement protection for members and the dependants of members. Membership of the Fund is voluntary, and upon joining, members are required to provide certain minimum information to the Trustees.

1.2 The Fund has members who are aged [#insert] respectively at the time of this document.

1.3 The personal assets of the members are as follows: [#insert list of assets, approximate value and any debt].

1.4 It is not intended that other members will be admitted to the fund. The current intention is for the members to receive a retirement benefit at the following ages: [#insert].

Benefits

1.5 The current intention is to pay [# lump sum, or pension] benefits upon retirement of the members. The Trustee shall invest Fund assets having regard to the need to realise the investments at the members' dates of retirement (or such later date as the member nominates in accordance with the rules governing the payment of benefits from complying superannuation funds).

1.6 There are no unallocated reserves in the fund and it is not intended to maintain any reserves.

Trustee Details

1.7 The Trustee of the Fund is [# insert] (Trustee) which company has 2 directors being the members.

2 Future Contributions

2.1 The members of the Fund will have sufficient death and disability cover provided through life cover in the Fund to enable the Trustees to take a long term perspective in setting the investment objectives of the Fund.

3 Past Investment Performance/Asset Mix

3.1 The past investment performance of the Fund has exceeded the CPI by [# insert]% over the last five years.

3.2 The assets of the fund are currently invested in the following proportions [# insert]:

a Public Company Shares

b Fixed Interest

c In-house Asset

4 Investment Objectives

General Objectives

4.1 The Trustee will at all times act prudently to pursue the maximum rate of return possible, subject to acceptable risk parameters, and the maintenance of appropriate diversification.

4.2 The Trustee will ensure that all investments are authorised under the trust deed, are made for the sole purpose of providing benefits to members and the dependants of members, and are made in accordance with the legislative requirements applicable to complying superannuation funds.

4.3 The Trustee will invest to ensure sufficient liquidity is retained within the Fund to meet benefit payments due, and will adjust its specific objectives where it believes the risk profile of the Fund has changed.

4.4 The Trustee will make investments in conjunction with members or any related parties only, the Principal Employer or on an arm's length basis, and in accordance with the in-house asset limits or any other legislative requirements.

Specific Objectives

4.5 Having considered the liability profile of the Fund, the Trustee has adopted the following objectives for the investment of the assets of the Fund:

a to achieve an investment return (net of tax and charges) that exceeds CPI by at least 4% per annum when measured over a rolling 10 year period;

b to achieve an investment return (net of tax and charges) that exceeds cash rates by at least 2% per annum when measured over a rolling 5 year period;

c to have a low expectation of negative returns in any 12 month period;

d to limit exposure to equities and property investment to under 70% of the assets of the Fund in order to limit earnings volatility; and

e to ensure the Fund generates sufficient cash flow to discharge administration expenses and other outgoings.

4.6 The Trustee will consider the implementation of these objectives through a single asset strategy where it considers that appropriate.

Review

4.7 The investment objectives of the Fund will be reviewed annually and at such other times as a significant event occurs which affects the Fund.

5 Investment Strategy

5.1 In order to achieve the investment objectives of the Fund, the Trustee wishes to adopt and pursue the strategy set out hereunder. The Trustee reserves the right to implement more than one strategy as it sees fit, and to offer separate strategies to members. The Trustee also reserves the right to implement separate and different action plans in the acquisition and disposal of assets pursuant to this strategy.

Diversification

5.2 The Trustee intends to achieve a level of diversification along the following parameters [#insert]:

Asset class	Range	Actual as at
Property (a) Unit trust and (b) direct	%	%
Equities Public company shares	%	%
Cash Cash management (a) Australian (b) International	%	%
Other assets (eg options, futures, art, collectibles etc)	%	%
TOTAL		

5.3 In considering the degree of diversification appropriate to the Fund, the Trustee has determined to take into account the following:

a the existing assets of the Fund;

b the existing personal assets of the members;

c its access to expert investment advice;

d the existing and projected membership and assets of the Fund; and

e the decision not to implement a reserving policy.

Fund Demographics

5.4 The Trustee has implemented its strategy taking into account the age of the members and their likely dates of retirement. It has also taken into account the expressed intention of the members to receive their benefits as [#insert - lump sums/allocated pensions] upon retirement.

Costs of investing

5.5 The Trustee will seek to minimise the investment costs it incurs, however at times upfront investment costs will be payable in order to obtain the best investment products that align with the Fund's overall investment strategy. The Trustee acknowledges that costs and penalties may also be part of the cost of implementing this investment strategy.

Performance Monitoring

5.6 To monitor the success of the investment policy in achieving the investment objectives, the Trustee will take the following steps:

a compare investment returns against investment objectives on an annual basis;

b compare the investment performance of the Fund against a sample group of superannuation master funds;

c compare investment returns against cash rates available over a 12 month period and will review this strategy on an annual basis or on such other basis as it believes appropriate.

Benchmarks

5.7 The Trustee will also measure the success of this investment strategy against certain benchmarks and indices. The nominated benchmarks for performance are:

a Australian shares - all ordinaries accumulation index;

b Liquid assets - average cash management trusts;

c Australian fixed trusts - commonwealth all series all maturities and accumulation index;

d Property trusts - average of composite property accumulation index; and

e In-house asset loans – average rates for comparable loans from major banks and legislative interest requirements.

Borrowing

5.8 The Trustee may, where consistent with the Fund's overall investment strategy, enter into limited recourse borrowing arrangements. Any decision by the Trustee to borrow funds must take the following factors into account:

a The risk involved in borrowing funds and holding an asset under a limited recourse borrowing arrangement;

b The likely return from the arrangement;

c The liquidity and cash flow consequences of entering into the arrangement;

d The time the members have until they retire;

e The impact of the arrangement on the Fund's cash flow requirements; and

f The investment risk tolerance of the members.

6 Asset Management Strategy

6.1 The Trustee will have regard to the following principles in the implementation of its investment strategy and the actual making of its investments.

6.2 The Trustee will specifically consider whether the unit trust it is intending to invest in is a fixed trust for tax purposes.

Unit Trusts

6.3 Prior to acquiring or disposing of any units in an unlisted unit trust the Trustee will obtain and consider property and rental valuations of all assets held by the unit trust to satisfy itself that the price of the units reflect true market values and constitutes a prudent investment/disposal on an arm's length basis.

6.4 The Trustee will also ascertain the intentions of the trustee of the unit trust in relation to borrowing (if any) and the use of the property as security.

Direct Property

6.5 Prior to acquiring or disposing of any property to be held directly by the Fund, the Trustee will obtain and consider property and rental valuations to satisfy itself that the price of the property reflects true market value and constitutes a prudent investment/disposal on an arm's length basis.

6.6 In obtaining a tenant (if any) for any property held by the Fund, the Trustee may enter into an associate, provided that a written lease agreement is made and the transaction is entered into on an arm's length basis with regular rental reviews.

6.7 In determining the proportion of Fund assets to be invested directly in property, the Trustee shall take into account the liability profile, diversification and liquidity requirements of the Fund.

Shares (Non-Associated Proprietary Companies)

6.8 Prior to acquiring (or disposing) of any shares in non-associated proprietary companies, the Trustee shall obtain a valuation to satisfy itself that the price of the shares reflect true market values and constitute a prudent investment/disposal.

6.9 The Trustee shall also take into account the saleability, security and dividend return of the shares and will ensure that the acquisition is not an in-house asset beyond acceptable limits or otherwise prohibited by legislation.

Shares (Public Company)

6.10 Prior to acquiring (or disposing) of any shares in public companies, the Trustee shall consider the portfolio profile of the Fund and the diversification of shareholding across different market sectors (industrial, retail, mining, agri business, financial, banking, etc.) with a view to attempting to obtain appropriate diversification.

6.11 The Trustee will also take into account any advice received in relation to expected capital growth and dividend income.

Debentures/First Mortgage

6.12 Prior to investing in any debenture/first mortgage the Trustee shall consider the period of investment, the security offered, the accessibility of funds, the return and likely interest rate movements.

Cash Management

6.13 Prior to investing or realising any cash management funds the Trustee shall consider the rate of return and security of such investment against the expected rate of return offered by alternative investments to cash (including, for example, fixed interest and bonds).

Artwork/Antiques/Collectibles

6.14 Prior to acquiring any collectibles as an investment of the Fund the Trustee will obtain an independent professional valuation from a qualified valuer and will ensure the asset represents a minor part of Fund assets. It will investigate future saleability of the asset and the likely price movements in future.

6.15 Prior to leasing any collectibles held by the Fund to any party the Trustee shall determine the commercial rental rate having regard to advice which the Trustee obtains from a qualified source. Any lease is only to be entered into under a written lease agreement made on an arm's length basis with obligations set out for full maintenance and insurance.

6.16 Prior to disposing of any collectibles held by the Fund, the

Trustee will obtain an independent professional valuation from a qualified valuer. The Trustee must also determine whether the proposed timing of the disposal is in the best interest of members having regard to the fluctuations in the value of the type of collectible of which the Trustee wishes to dispose.

In-House Assets

6.17 The Trustee will only acquire in-house assets if permitted under legislation governing complying superannuation funds and if the Trustee determines that it is in the best interest of members.

Financial Derivatives

6.18 The Trustee will develop a separate specific investment strategy if any form of financial derivative is to be acquired by the Fund, including:

- **a** options;
- **b** futures;
- **c** foreign currency;
- **d** swaps;
- **e** crowd source lending;
- **f** contracts for the difference (CFDs);
- **g** structured or synthetic bonds or shares.

7 Insurance

7.1 The Trustee will regularly consider whether the Fund should hold insurance cover for its members and based on an analysis of the needs of the members, cash flow requirements for the Fund and the insurance already held by the members outside of the Fund, the following insurance was considered appropriate for the Trustee to obtain [# insert]:

Member	Insurance type	Amount

The above investment strategy has been prepared with reference to the checklist set out in the Schedule to this document is confirmed by the Trustee on [#insert].

[# insert signing provisions for Trustee]

Fund Investments Involving Associated Persons and Entities

SIS Requirements

Prohibition Against Acquisition of Assets from Related Parties

Is the asset to be acquired from a 'related party' (as defined under SIS) of the Fund?

Is the asset which is being acquired business real property of a related party of a member?

If yes, all of the following requirements must be satisfied:

a the asset must be acquired at market value;
b after the acquisition of the property all property acquired from the related party may be up to 100% of the total value of the assets of the Fund; and
c the acquisition must be a freehold or leasehold interest in real property used wholly or exclusively in a business.

Is the asset which is being acquired a listed security?

If yes, it must be acquired at market value.

Transactions involving use of interposed entities. These should be vetted by professional advisers to ensure that they are not caught by the anti-avoidance provisions of SIS.

Arm's Length Basis Requirement

Is the transaction being entered into on an arm's length basis?

This requirement is satisfied if the terms of the transaction taken as a whole are no more or less favourable to either party than would be the case if it involved arm's length parties.

In-house Asset Rules

Does the investment involve a loan to or an investment in a related parry or related trust of the Fund or an asset of the Fund subject to a lease or lease arrangement between the Fund and a related party? If so, the level of such investments should not exceed 5% of the market value of the Fund.

Prepare action plan to monitor level of such investments to ensure that the level is regularly monitored, in line with Part 8 of SIS.

Unit trust and other complex structures or transactions should be vetted by professional advisers for possible breaches of the in-house asset rules.

Loans and Financial Assistance to Members and their Relatives

Does the investment involve a loan to a member, relative or associate of a member? If so, such an investment is not permitted.

Consider whether the investment involves giving financial assistance to the member, relative or associate of a member. If so, such an investment should not be made.

Prudential Requirements

The Trustee should obtain an independent valuation of the asset from a qualified person.

If the non-arm's length person from whom the asset is to be acquired is a trustee or a director of the trustee company, full disclosure should be made to the co-trustees/co-directors, of the nature of the individual's interest in the asset. If possible, the person should not take part in the Trustee's deliberations regarding the acquisition of the asset.

The acquisition of the asset must conform with the current investment objectives and strategy of the Fund.

The transaction should be thoroughly documented and minuted and deposits/purchase moneys must be paid.

In determining the market price of any shares to be acquired the Trustee should take into account whether the purchase is "ex dividend" or "cum dividend". Similarly with unit trust acquisitions, the purchase price should reflect any income distribution available.

Appointment of Fund Investment Manager
Questions To Be Used In The Selection Criteria Of An Investment Manager

Organisational Issues

1. What is ownership structure of investment manager?
2. What is the management structure?
3. Does the investment manager have an office in the same city as Trustee? If not, how will it service the Fund?
4. What are the business objectives of the investment manager?
5. How long has the company been in business in Australia?
6. Are there any potential conflicts of interest? If so how are these dealt with?
7. What other affiliated services can the investment manager provide (custodial, brokerage etc.).
8. Does the investment manager have adequate professional indemnity insurance cover?

Resources

1. Who are the people to be involved in the provision of investment advisory services?
2. What role will these people be playing with the Fund?
3. What data base and other analysis facilities does the investment manager have and what will be available for the Fund?
4. What types of research does the investment manager carry out and how does it go about it?

Fees

1. On what basis are fees charged?
2. What is the breakup of fees on entry, management, and exit?
3. How often are fees reviewed and what advice is provided on review?

Appendix Three

NON-BINDING DEATH BENEFIT NOMINATIONS

Nominated beneficiaries

I nominate the following people as my Nominated Beneficiaries and confirm my understanding that this nomination is not binding on the Trustee of the SMSF:

Name	Relationship to member (delete all but the one that is applicable)	Total benefit (%)– must total 100%
	spouse/child/a person who is financially dependent on me/ legal personal representative	%
	spouse/child/a person who is financially dependent on me/ legal personal representative	%
	spouse/child/a person who is financially dependent on me/ legal personal representative	%
	spouse/child/a person who is financially dependent on me/ legal personal representative	%
		100%

Date

Signature of

Appendix Four

BINDING DEATH BENEFIT NOMINATIONS

Binding nomination

I, ________________________, being a member of the Fund, direct that the trustee of the Fund is to pay any benefits in respect of my membership of the Fund on or after my death as follows:

> User note: include applicable nomination and delete options that are not applicable

100% of my benefit to my legal personal representative for distribution under the terms of my will.

OR

100% of my benefit as set out in the table below:

Full name of nominated beneficiary	Relationship to member (delete all but the one that is applicable)	Percentage (must total 100%)
	spouse/child/a person who is financially dependent on me/legal personal representative	%
	spouse/child/a person who is financially dependent on me/legal personal representative	%
	spouse/child/a person who is financially dependent on me/legal personal representative	%
	spouse/child/a person who is financially dependent on me/legal personal representative	%
		100%

Confirmation

I confirm:

a if any person named in the table immediately above does not survive me, or dies before the whole of the relevant benefit is paid to them, then the share of the benefit to which they would otherwise have been entitled (or any part of the benefit that remains unpaid) must be paid to my legal personal representative for distribution under the terms of my will;

b my understanding that each anticipated payment of benefits in this nomination is permitted under the trust deed and the *Superannuation Industry (Supervision) Act 1993 (Cth)* (**Act**);

c this nomination revokes any previous nomination (of any kind) I may have made in relation to my benefits in the Fund;

d this nomination will only terminate if expressly revoked by me in writing; and

e each witness is at least 18 years or older and is not a nominated beneficiary.

Signing

On the date of ______________________________

and in the presence of the First Witness and the Second Witness, I sign this binding death benefit nomination in relation to my benefits in the Fund

____

Full signature of member

The member signed this binding death benefit nomination in our presence and we have also signed in the presence of the member, and each other, with all of

_________________________	_________________________
Full signature of First Witness	Full signature of Second Witness
_________________________	_________________________
Full name (capitals)	Full name (capitals)
_________________________	_________________________
Occupation	Occupation
_________________________	_________________________
Suburb/State	Suburb/State

Important notes

As a member of the Fund it is your own responsibility to ensure that the proposed payment of benefits in this nomination complies with the Act.

You should obtain specialist advice before signing the nomination in relation to:

a whether a nominated beneficiary is permitted to receive your benefits under the Act; and

b the taxation consequences of the payment of your benefits to your nominated beneficiaries.

c There is other important information provided to members about this nomination in an information sheet that the trustee of the Fund can provide to you.

Appendix Five

INFORMATION SHEET - BDBN

Overview

UNDER THE *SUPERANNUATION Industry (Supervision) Act* 1993 (Cth) (**Act**), the trustee is required to give you the information that it believes you need to understand your rights to require the trustee to pay your member benefits under the Fund.

The required information is set out below.

Nomination alternatives

Under the Act, a member can require the trustee of the Fund to pay benefits in a certain way on their death.

There are essentially six possible scenarios in relation to any death benefit payment and these are summarised below. A reference to BDBN means **Binding Death Benefit Nomination**.

a. no nomination - the member may have made no direction or nomination to the Trustee. In this situation, the Trustee has complete discretion as to how to distribute the death benefit payment;
b. non-BDBN – if the member has made a nomination which does not satisfy the requirements of a BDBN, the Trustee retains complete discretion as to how to distribute the death benefit, although it should still take into account what is set out in the non BDBN;
c. lapsing BDBN – where there is a valid BDBN, the Trustee must pay the death benefit in accordance with it. The only situation where the Trustee need not follow the lapsing BDBN is where, even though it is otherwise validly prepared, it is stated to be enforceable for a defined period (often three years). If the member dies outside the relevant period, then the Trustee is not bound to follow the BDBN;

d non lapsing BDBN – it is possible for members to create BDBNs that are non-lapsing. If they are validly prepared, they are binding on the Trustee;
e superannuation will – a BDBN can be embedded into the trust deed for the Fund. Specialist advice should be obtained in relation to this approach, which is generally adopted where there are concerns that a nomination may not be followed; and
f reversionary beneficiary – where a member has been receiving an income stream, it is possible to establish that income stream in a way that it automatically reverts or passes to another person, regardless of any nomination that may have been made.

The interplay between death benefit payments and a member's estate plan can be complex and best practice dictates that members should implement a comprehensive estate plan and complementary strategy in relation to their superannuation entitlements.

The impact of incapacity should also be considered. For example, if a lapsing BDBN is to be implemented, thought should be given to allowing your legal personal representative to have the power to sign an updated BDBN on your behalf.

Requirements for BDBNs

Any BDBN must comply with the requirements set out in the template nomination provided by the Fund.

These requirements include:

a the form of the nomination;
b clear direction as to who is to receive what benefit; and
c that the intended recipient is a 'dependant' as defined under the Act (a dependant includes - spouse, any child of the member (regardless of age), and any person who is financially dependent on the member) or your legal personal representative (as defined under the Act).

Trust Deed

The trust deed for the Fund must allow for BDBNs to be given to the trustee. The trust deed for the Fund does currently have the required provisions.

Advantages of BDBNs

Three of the main advantages of BDBNs are:

a. reduced risk of successful disputes over death benefit payments;
b. tax planning opportunities for members with infant children; and
c. asset protection planning.

Disadvantages of BDBNS

Three of the main disadvantages of BDBNs are:

a. the tax and estate planning issues in relation to the payment of superannuation death benefits are complex and difficulties can often arise with BDBNs that prove to be inappropriate;
b. if a member's circumstances change and they have failed to update their BDBN, the original BDBN will remain binding on the trustee; and
c. a number of court decisions since 2012 have resulted in significant confusion about the exact requirements to ensure a BDBN is valid.

Process from here

If you have doubts about if any aspect of an intended BDBN, you must obtain specialist advice before signing the nomination.

About the Author

Matthew Burgess is one of the four directors and founders of specialist firm View Legal.

Having the opportunity to help clients achieve their goals is what he is most passionate about.

As Matthew always works in conjunction with trusted advisers (whether it be accountants, financial advisers or other lawyers) and their clients, finding ways to fundamentally improve the value received by those advisers, and in turn their clients, has led him to develop numerous game changing models.

Examples include providing guaranteed upfront fixed pricing, founding what is widely regarded as Australia's first virtual law firm, and more recently, developing a platform that gives advisers access to market leading advice and support for less than $1 a week.

Matthew's specialisation in tax, structuring, asset protection, estate and succession planning has seen him recognised by most leading industry associations including the Tax Institute, the Weekly Tax Bulletin and since 2014 in the Australian 'Best Lawyers' list for trusts and estates.

Work is one aspect of his life Matthew loves, so there is no need to be constantly searching for 'balance'. His other great loves are:

- Family — they are profiled in various ways through the series of children's books he has written under the pseudonym 'Lily Burgess' — see www.wordsfromdaddysmouth.com.au and various TV commercials;

2. Learning — going cold Turkey on television and most forms of media in late 2005 (the reasons for this are a story for another time) has radically increased Matthew's ability to study the great authors and inspired him to publish a book that explores the concept of 'true success' — see www.thedreamenabler.com.au
3. Health — aside from being a foodie and swimming at least a 5km a week, Matthew installed a stand up workstation in 2007 and among a few other lifestyle choices, it changed his life.